Unforgiven

**Edward
Buscombe**

First published in 2004 by the
British Film Institute
21 Stephen Street, London W1T 1LN

Copyright © Edward Buscombe 2004

The British Film Institute promotes greater
understanding and appreciation of,
and access to, film and moving image
culture in the UK.

British Library Cataloguing-in-Publication Data
A catalogue record for this book is available
from the British Library

ISBN 1-84457-033-9

Series design by Andrew Barron
& Collis Clements Associates

Typeset in Italian Garamond and Swiss 721BT
by D R Bungay Associates, Burghfield, Berks

Printed in Great Britain by
Norwich Colour Print, Drayton, Norfolk

BFI Modern Classics

Rob W...
Serie...

BFI Modern Classics is a series of critical studies of films produced over the last three decades. Writers explore their chosen films, offering a range of perspectives on the dominant art and entertainment medium in contemporary culture. The series gathers together snapshots of our passion for and understanding of recent movies.

Also Published

Groundhog Day
Ryan Gilbey

Nosferatu – Phantom der Nacht
S.S. Prawer

Withnail & I
Kevin Jackson

(see a full list of titles in the series
at the back of this book)

Clint Eastwood during the filming of *Unforgiven*

Contents

Acknowledgments

Thanks to Noel King for locating the script and other advice, to Christopher Frayling and Jim Kitses for several conversations, to Clyde Jeavons for a poster and to David Webb Peoples for a phone call. Thanks also to Rob White for his astute editing.

One of the UK release posters

Unforgiven

1

Unforgiven opens as it closes, with a sunset. Outlined against the red sky, a man is digging a grave beside a lonely shack on the prairie, beneath a solitary tree. Sunsets have a special resonance in the Western. It's the time of day by which you have to get out of town or else, a tradition that goes back at least as far as Owen Wister's seminal novel, *The Virginian*, first published in 1903. In 'Duel at Sundown', the title of a 1959 episode of the TV series *Maverick* in which Clint

Sunset and autumnal leaves

Eastwood appeared as a boastful gunslinger, he gives James Garner just such an ultimatum. But there's more to it than that. The sun sets, after all, in the west; that's the direction across the map the pioneers are always travelling, but it's also metaphorically the direction we're all travelling ('We all have it coming, Kid'). One way or another, Westerns are always about death.

Hence the mood of melancholy with which so many of them are tinged. But this may also derive from the fact that Westerns are set in the past, a past that is gone for ever, cannot be recovered, and so there is often a sense that something has been lost. In the 1960s the mood of nostalgia deepened. Robert Aldrich went so far as to make a picture called *The Last Sunset* (1961), a title that doubly emphasises that sense of something passing. The following year Sam Peckinpah's *Ride the High Country* (1962) set the tone for much of what was to follow later in the decade. Two ageing gunfighters, played by veteran Western actors Randolph Scott and Joel McCrea, get together for one last mission. The west is changing, leaving them behind, relics of an earlier, more chivalrous era. At the end of the film McCrea is shot in a heroic gunfight. As he lies dying the camera cranes upwards to the golden yellow autumn leaves of the Sierras, a metaphor no less elegiac than a sunset. There's an echo of this autumnal foliage in a beautiful lyrical scene early in *Unforgiven*, when Ned and Will have just joined up with the Kid and the three ride through a lush and verdant landscape where the trees are turning red and gold, a magical moment before the darkness and storms that lie in store.

During the 1960s, nostalgia extended from regret at the passing of the west towards the genre itself. The production of Westerns in Hollywood fell steeply, down to a mere eleven in 1963, barely 10 per cent of what it had been ten years earlier. For a time this decline was masked by the unexpected phenomenon of the Italian Western, in which, as everyone knows, Clint Eastwood made his name as The Man with No Name. John Ford, informed by fellow Western director Burt Kennedy that Westerns were now being made in Italy, could only respond 'You're kidding.'[1] But the several hundred spaghetti Westerns made in the middle of the 1960s helped revive Hollywood's own contribution, not so much in terms of absolute numbers, which remained stuck at an annual figure of twenty or so, but in terms of themes and styles. Peckinpah's *The Wild Bunch*, coming at the end of the decade, is inconceivable without the stylised violence and ideological disillusion of Sergio Leone's films.

Yet the revival was temporary. As the 1970s progressed, the Western slipped to the margins of Hollywood production. There may be many reasons for this. Audience demographics were changing, with younger filmgoers finding the genre old-fashioned compared to science fiction or the newly reinvigorated horror film. The death or retirement of the genre's greatest stars accelerated the decline. *Ride the High Country* had been Randolph Scott's last performance. None of the other major stars continued beyond the 1970s. Henry Fonda's last Western was an Italian production, *Il mio nome è Nessuno*, in 1973. John Wayne and James Stewart made their last Western together, *The Shootist*, in 1976. It was directed by Don Siegel, and its story, of an elderly gunfighter who knows he is dying, could scarcely be more appropriate, either

John Wayne in *The Shootist* (Don Siegel / Dino de Laurentiis, 1976)

to Wayne's own career (he was in fact dying of cancer at the time) or to the melancholy mood of the genre.[2]

The ideological framework within which the Western has had to work has shifted markedly since John Ford's high-water mark in the mid-1950s; already by the 1970s many of its certainties were being undermined. In particular, the central figure of the hero, confident in his masculinity and physical prowess, the man who knows what a man's gotta do, was threatened by an alliance of forces, of which feminism was only the most directly challenging. Even in the 1950s deep-seated faults in the bedrock of American society were causing cracks to appear in the previously impregnable carapace of the male hero. In the remarkable series of Westerns directed by Anthony Mann and starring James Stewart, beginning with *Winchester '73* in 1950, the Western hero is a troubled figure, in the grip of powerful, even irrational obsessions, his emotions barely under control. In the middle of the decade, John Ford's magisterial *The Searchers* (1956) cast John Wayne, the embodiment of all that was most dependable and uncomplicated, as a man driven near to madness by his hatreds. Even works by lesser directors, such as Edward Dmytryk's *Warlock* (1959), featured heroes, in this case the saintly Henry Fonda, whose motivations were complex and actions not always admirable.

John Wayne in *The Searchers* (John Ford / C. V. Whitney Pictures, 1956)

By the 1970s, heroism itself seemed a troubled concept. Westerns were now full of anti-heroes such as the comic figure of Jack Crabb in *Little Big Man* (1970), forever changing sides in an attempt to avoid confrontations. Robert Altman's demythologising *Buffalo Bill and the Indians* (1976) exposed the venality and cynicism involved in the creation of William Frederick Cody, who first saw the full possibilities of the west as a commodity, as packaged entertainment. Mel Brooks's irreverent satire, *Blazing Saddles* (1974), sent up the whole genre. There had been parodies before, but they had been affectionate; for Brooks nothing was sacred. The historical foundations of the genre also came under systematic attack in films that debunked the real-life figures that previous decades had so assiduously built up. In *Doc* (1971) it was Wyatt Earp and Doc Holliday, in *Dirty Little Billy* (1972) Billy the Kid, in *The Great Northfield Minnesota Raid* (1972) it was Jesse James.

In the parallel field of the history of the west, the triumphalist version of western history informed by the notion of manifest destiny, the idea that the white race had a God-given right, even a duty, to expand into the lands which it misleadingly called 'virgin' but which were already the preserve of native or Latino peoples, was already being questioned in the 1970s. Possibly this was propelled by events in Vietnam, which undermined America's imperialist ambitions. In 1987 Patricia Nelson Limerick's *The Legacy of Conquest* mounted a full-scale assault upon the theories of westward expansion that had so far dominated the field and which originated in the so-called 'frontier thesis', first formulated by Frederick Jackson Turner in 1893. Limerick charged that this account (which saw America's social and political virtues, identified as adaptability, ingenuity and energy, as deriving from the free and easy life of the frontier) left out a great deal, in particular the contribution of women and of ethnic minority groups, and was over-celebratory, ignoring much in the history of the west that was shameful or disastrous.

In this context, it seemed, only Clint Eastwood had the necessary star power and vitality to ensure the Western's survival. From his first leading role in a Hollywood Western, *Hang 'Em High* in 1968, he was to

Hang 'Em High
(Ted Post / Leonard
Freeman Productions,
Malpaso, 1968)

make a total of ten Westerns up to *Pale Rider* in 1985. If this could scarcely compare with the productivity of earlier stars (Randolph Scott made no less than thirty-nine Westerns between 1945 and 1962), it meant nevertheless that Eastwood was almost single-handedly carrying the genre upon his shoulders.[3]

There is hardly space to trace in detail Eastwood's career as a Western hero,[4] but what is most striking, beyond the deepening of the actor's and director's craft that has marked his progression, is the extent

Josey with entourage in *The Outlaw Josey Wales* (Clint Eastwood / Warner Bros. / Warner Home Video, Malpaso, 1976)

to which he has been alert to the shifts of tone and perspective which have been forced upon the genre over the past third of a century, as the result of changes both within the cinema and without.

As the above dates suggest, the Western film was in some respects in advance of the historians on the question of manifest destiny, having already done something to redress past imbalances in respect of the Indians and other ethnic groups, and readily acknowledging that the west was often a dark and dirty place. Eastwood's Westerns were alert to these currents from an early date. As we shall see, the role of women in his films, including his Westerns, underwent a subtle development over time. But in other respects too his films did not simply recycle the traditional versions of the Western myth. In *The Outlaw Josey Wales* (1976) Eastwood as the eponymous hero, starting as a loner, as Western heroes traditionally are, gradually collects around him a disparate group of individuals, who include several women, an elderly Cherokee with a delightfully ironic take on the role of the Indian, and a stray dog. *Bronco Billy* (1980), set in the

Bronco Billy (Clint Eastwood / Warner Bros., Second Street Films, 1980)

(Overleaf) Little Bill is confronted by Alice

present day, has Eastwood playing the owner of a wild west show whose innocent, even childish belief in 'Western' values is tested almost to destruction by the cynicism of those around him. In *Pale Rider*, Eastwood's last Western before *Unforgiven*, his role is certainly heroic, leading a group of gold-miners in their struggle against a heartless corporation. But there is something ultimately unhealthy about the hero-worship he attracts, in particular from a young girl who convinces herself she is in love with him, while in its focus on hydraulic mining and the damage it does to the environment, the film echoes the increasing consensus of the 'new western historians' that economic development in the west was frequently rapacious and destructive.

What all these films indicate is that Eastwood has been alive to the changing social milieu in which the Western had to make its way since 1970. One could not simply reproduce the old certainties, whether of masculine or white supremacy, or of progress. If the Western was to continue to be viable, it would need to be adapted to contemporary sensibilities, show that it was aware of its own past and in touch with the present. And that is precisely what *Unforgiven* tries to do, by turns drawing strength from the roots of the genre, the accreted meanings of character and convention, but then always inflecting them, adapting them, subverting them to refashion the genre into something viable for the modern age.

Hydraulic mining in *Pale Rider* (Clint Eastwood / Malpaso, Warner Bros. / Warner Home Video, 1985)

2

Whose grave is being dug in the opening scene? Over the image comes a crawler:

She was a comely young woman and not without prospects. Therefore it was heartbreaking to her mother that she would enter into marriage with William Munny, a known thief and murderer, a man of notoriously vicious and intemperate disposition.

When she died it was not at his hands as her mother might have expected, but of smallpox. That was 1878.

The language is deliberately, self-consciously archaic ('comely', 'intemperate disposition'). Is this intended to impart a certain documentary veracity by speaking in a nineteenth-century idiom? Since the 1960s large numbers of personal testaments, diaries and other written accounts of the historical west have been published, allowing us to experience the settlement of the west in the actual words of those who lived it. *Unforgiven* goes to great lengths to evoke the period in its careful choice of costumes and sets, or in historical references such as the assassination of President Garfield. But it does so in a manner that seems to call attention to itself, not quite pastiche, but not quite realism either. The language of this opening text, its over-elaborate Victorianism, its artificiality, indicates something besides a desire for authenticity. It's as if the real west is now so far distant from us that to summon it into existence requires a kind of antiquarianism. It implies that by 1992 the Western genre itself was a museum piece, something that could only be resurrected by a certain form of arch knowingness. We know this language is quaint, it says, and we know the Western is a historical relic; it's this very quality we wish to emphasise right from the beginning, and then we'll show you how to bring it up to date.

This use of language extends into the dialogue, which is also, if not archaic, then slightly stilted by the rhythms and vocabulary of the past. There's a measured formality even in the heat of the moment, as in Little Bill Daggett's exhortation to his deputies in the final confrontation in the saloon:

'All right, gentlemen, he's got one barrel left. When he fires that take out your pistols and shoot him down like the mangy scoundrel he is.' Most of the principal characters in the film speak in this manner, slightly pedantic and self-conscious. It's as though they are acting their parts, deliberately giving them weight and sonority. As we shall see, all of them, even the hero himself, finally, want to participate in a kind of myth-making.

3

The next scene is a rude contrast, plunging us directly into the mundane, the immediate, the everyday, rubbing our face in it, in fact. A man and a woman are having awkward, ungraceful sex in a murky, sordid room. Their enjoyment is interrupted by cries from the next room, and we see a woman menaced, then attacked with a knife by a customer. It's soon apparent the violence is wholly undeserved. (How could you deserve to be disfigured for life?)

What could be more contemporary, shocking yet banal, than such a scene of sexual violence? The assault is occasioned by male insecurity, a vicious reaction to a prostitute's mockery of a client's penis, delivering a brutal answer to a question so often now posed in irony: does size matter? From the beginning we have issues raised which seem more immediate to our own age than to the Victorian era in which the film is set: male fears about the loss of power, engendering violence against women.

What should women do about these threats? A year before *Unforgiven* was released Hollywood confronted some of these issues in *Thelma & Louise* (1991), set in contemporary times, in which two women go on the rampage following the attempted rape of one of them. Predictably, the film provoked outcries from male spectators, anxious at the hostility and the counter-violence the film seemed to express.

Women can't very plausibly go on the rampage in 1880. The friends of the mutilated prostitute will have to find another route to justice. In the next scene a debate follows about what would constitute an appropriate response to the shocking attack on poor Delilah. The issue of violence against women may be highly contemporary, but questions of the law are

traditional in the Western, which, classically, is set on the frontier, that line between civilisation and the wilderness, the point at which the struggle between the two is still in progress, the issue still in doubt. This goal, of overcoming the savagery which the wilderness harbours in order that civilisation may be established, must be achieved through the institution of the law, whether civil or military. But, paradoxically, law and order can only be achieved through the application of necessary violence, a violence that, unlike the brutality of outlaws or savages, is legitimated and, to use Richard Slotkin's term, regenerative.[5] Westerns recount time and again the courage of the soldier who must fight against hostiles who would dispute the advance of civilisation, or the bravery of the lawman who must stand up against outlawry and make the streets safe for women and children. The violence which they deal out is sanctioned; its application allows peace to flourish, even though the man who administers it may not always, because of his albeit temporary regression to a more primitive state, find a place for himself within the order he has established.

Little Bill Daggett, the sheriff of Big Whiskey, is more concerned with keeping the peace and upholding the law than with abstract notions of justice. Daggett at first proposes violent retribution in the form of a whipping for the two young men accused of the crime, a kind of punishment, we later learn, he has a taste for. It's cheap, immediate and the matter will be quickly resolved. But Skinny, the proprietor of the

Delilah (Anna Thomson) after the attack

saloon where the prostitutes are employed, offers a little lesson in capitalist economics, phrased in terms a Marxist could not better. He regards the women as his property. He has invested money in bringing them out to this isolated spot. The women have no value to him except insofar as their looks can be exchanged for cash. Now his goods are damaged, and he wants recompense, not justice or even revenge: 'nobody's going to pay good money for a cut-up whore'.

The women are thus doubly wronged, first by the act of violence itself, then by being assigned the status of chattels. The law, which ought to give them justice, at first offers a minimal revenge, but then Little Bill sides with Skinny and his property rights. The cowboys must pay a fine of seven horses, payable not to the woman wronged but to her owner. When Strawberry Alice, the leader of the prostitutes, protests that the punishment is insufficient, Little Bill explains that the cowboys are not bad men, just 'hard-working boys that was foolish', not 'given over to wickedness in a regular way'. 'Like whores?' Alice retorts. It's one law for respectable men, if they do attack women, and another for the Delilahs of this world. Little Bill, as we shall see, is all for respectability.

Living in a society in which women's rights are minimal but where money talks (though ironically Wyoming, where the film is set, was the first state in the Union to give women the vote, in 1869), the prostitutes' only means to empower themselves is by buying justice, and so they decide to hire gunmen to act for them; they want personal vengeance; an eye for an eye, or more; in effect capital punishment but outside the law, a life in exchange for a disfiguration. Both cowboys involved in the attack are eventually murdered at the women's instigation, though one clearly has had only a minimal involvement and shows remorse. Yet though the roles of all the men involved in the unfolding of events, both heroes and villains, come under severe scrutiny, there's never any overt criticism of the women's actions. Implicitly, the film sides with these women. It does not question their right to do what they do, only the motives and actions of those who perform on their behalf.

In this respect, *Unforgiven* seems to go against the grain of the genre. The Western is not celebrated for favouring women. Traditionally, there's a limited range of roles on offer (young marriageable girl, wife, schoolteacher, whore), all of them subordinate. It might be argued this is a necessary consequence of creating a reasonably plausible picture of the past; what other roles were in fact available to women on the frontier? Well, actually quite a few, as the researches of historians have shown.[6] It is true that you can't plausibly show women in the middle of the nineteenth century behaving like modern feminists, but in actuality women did often play active roles. But there's more to the secondary status of women in the genre than historical accuracy. In its heyday (say from 1939 to 1960) the Western had too much invested in masculinity and its discontents to spend much time on what women want. In the classic narrative, law and order can only be imposed by a strong man who is prepared to pit his masculinity against other men, that is, he is willing to use at least the necessary minimum of violence. But strength comes always at a price. The hero suffers stress, anxiety, doubts and setbacks. Masculinity is tested to the limit and sometimes beyond. In

Geraldine Page and Eastwood in *The Beguiled* (Don Siegel / Universal Pictures, Malpaso, 1970)

such an extreme world women, though often the ostensible reason why the man struggles to impose the law, are regarded as little more than a distraction.

In *Unforgiven*, however, it is the women who initiate the action and call the shots as it were, who set the ball rolling by their demands for justice. If this is novel in the Western, it was by no means a departure for Clint Eastwood. True, women are largely absent from the trio of Westerns Eastwood made with Sergio Leone and which made him into an international star. In his Hollywood films they play a much more pivotal role, even if in the early films they are often menacing figures, like the scorned and mentally deranged woman in Eastwood's first film as director, *Play Misty for Me* (1971), or the murderous harpies who hold him captive in *The Beguiled* (1971). There are good, strong roles for women in later films, such as the gutsy Gus in *The Gauntlet* (1977), played by Eastwood's long-term partner Sondra Locke, or the staunchly feminist Beryl in *Tightrope* (1984), played by Geneviève Bujold. In *Pale Rider* Carrie Snodgress is Sarah, a complex character drawn to the hero but wary of him. As the women's roles got

Sondra Locke in *The Gauntlet* (Clint Eastwood / Malpaso, Warner Bros., 1977)

Geneviève Bujold in *Tightrope* (Richard Tuggle / Warner Bros., Malpaso, 1984)

more rewarding, Eastwood's own screen persona acquired a new vulnerability: the deeply troubled cop in *Tightrope*, the flawed and drunken country singer in *Honkytonk Man* (1982), the tragic Hemingwayesque figure of Wilson in *White Hunter, Black Heart* (1990), the heartbroken lover in *The Bridges of Madison County* (1995). Often too, the hero is the butt of comedy, with feisty women making jokes at his expense. No one would claim Eastwood for feminism, but by the

Rene Russo and Eastwood in *In the Line of Fire* (Wolfgang Petersen / Columbia Pictures, Castle Rock Entertainment, Apple/Rose / Columbia Tristar Home Entertainment, 1993)

early 1990s his films had come a long way from the straightforward macho attitudes of *Dirty Harry* (1971). Eastwood has always been a canny player in the industry. When muscle men like Sylvester Stallone and Arnold Schwarzenegger were flaunting their torsos in the early 1980s with movies like the initial Rambo film, *First Blood* (1982) and *Conan the Barbarian* (1981), Eastwood had already moved on to *Bronco Billy*, an ironic take on the whole myth of the Western. By the time of *In the Line of Fire* (1993), when the Eastwood character shows a lack of respect for the presence of female agents in the secret service, agent Rene Russo is allowed to refer to him as a dinosaur.

Eastwood is sufficiently alert to the issues raised by the representation of women in the cinema that for the prostitutes he did not cast a bevy of typical busty Hollywood starlets. The chief spokeswoman of the little group, Strawberry Alice, is played by Frances Fisher. Eastwood had first cast her in his film *Pink Cadillac* in 1989. They had begun an affair, which resulted in the birth of a child. The relationship did not last beyond 1995, but Eastwood gave her a small part in his later film, *True Crime* (1999). Fisher, though appealing, is not a conventional beauty, nor is Anna Thomson, who plays the unfortunate Delilah. Going against the conventions in the casting helps give the film both authenticity (this is what prostitutes might really have looked like) and credibility with the female audience (these characters are sympathetic, not bimbos).

Frances Fisher as Alice

4

There's an uncommon lot of writing appearing on the screen in this picture. After the crawler comes the place and date of the action, information often provided at the start of a Western to anchor it chronologically and topographically: 'Big Whiskey Wyoming, 1880'. Soon we see the headstone of William Munny's wife ('Claudia Feathers Munny Born Mar. 11 1849 Died Aug. 6 1878 Aged 29 years'). The town of Big Whiskey is plastered with signs: Blacksmith; Undertaker; Tailor: Cutting and Fitting; Greelys Saloon (sans apostrophe); Carpenter; Restaurant; Barber; Chinese Laundry, Dry Goods and Clothing; Sheriff). In the saloon are more signs: 'No Firearms' and 'No Credit', and inside the sheriff's office are the usual Wanted posters. Outside of town is the sheriff's sign to check your guns: 'No Fire Arms in Big Whiskey Ordinance 14 Deposit pistols & rifles County Office'. (There's a different version of this sign as Will and Ned arrive in Big Whiskey; a continuity lapse, or are they on the other side of town?) On the train that brings English Bob (whose carriages are marked 'Northwestern Railroad') people are reading newspapers: the *Omaha Evening Express* and the *Cheyenne Gazette* ('President Garfield in Critical Condition'). Later we see the book written by W. W. Beauchamp, *The Duke of Death* (aka *The Duck of Death*). Then there's the notice attached to Ned's dead body: 'this is what happens to assassins around here'. And at the end of the picture comes the final part of the crawler, of which more anon.

Written authority

What's all this writing for? Of course it has an indexical function, giving us useful information. And it gives a feel of time and place, lends a certain authenticity, just as the slightly stilted dialogue does. But there's more to it than that. Sometimes the writing attempts to record facts, pin them down, as in Beauchamp's literary efforts, seeking to arrive at a correct and convincing version of events. Or the writing is an attempt at imposing order, the sheriff's ordinances stamping his authority on the town. Unfortunately for both Beauchamp and Little Bill, the truth proves elusive, even deceitful, and authority can be challenged.

5

After the scenes in Big Whiskey we cut to a ramshackle corral on a windswept plain, where a gaunt and poorly dressed middle-aged man is wrestling with some pigs while his children look on. Western heroes don't usually have children, not Gary Cooper in *High Noon* (1952) nor Ethan Edwards in *The Searchers*, not James Stewart in *The Man from Laramie* (1955) nor the hero of *Shane* (1953). Kids tie you down, even more than a wife. Nor do heroes keep pigs. And they certainly don't get down in the shit.[7]

One of the most pleasurable things about *Unforgiven* is the variety of different ways it finds to inflect a story that is in essence as generic as they come: a retired gunfighter is called out of retirement to do one last job. Ageing is a common enough theme in the Western. In Henry King's *The*

Gregory Peck in *The Gunfighter*
(Henry King / Twentieth Century-Fox, 1950)

Gunfighter (1950) Gregory Peck is Jimmy Ringo, a gunman who is looking to finally settle down. He's weary of the wandering life. Tragically, just at the moment he has made his decision, he's gunned down by just the sort of glory-hunting little punk he has been trying to avoid. In *The Searchers* John Wayne as Ethan is self-conscious about his age ('No need to call me sir, either, nor grandpa, nor Methuselah'). Both *Ride the High Country* and *The Shootist*, as we've seen, explore this theme, and in *Monte Walsh* (1970) Lee Marvin and Jack Palance are two ageing cowboys threatened by unemployment. So having Eastwood play a character who may be too old for heroics is not a novel idea. What's fresh is the ingenuity and subtlety with which it is played out.

Eastwood was over sixty when he made *Unforgiven*, and for the first time, perhaps, he looks his age. He has an emaciated look, the skin stretched tight on his face and the thinning hair greying and wispy. The film goes to some length to emphasise just how unheroic he is. A rider suddenly appears when Eastwood, or William Munny as we should now call him, is floundering in the pig pen, and announces himself as the Schofield Kid. From the start he is doubtful of Munny's credentials: 'You don't look like no rootin', tootin' son of a bitch and cold-blooded assassin,' he says to the dirty, bedraggled figure of the pig farmer. The Kid has a hyperbolic vision of what the west is like, or should be like. Munny disappoints him.

'You don't look like no rootin', tootin' son of a bitch'

The Kid explains the deal; the prostitutes of Big Whiskey have pooled their money to pay someone to avenge them. He invites Munny to join him in collecting the reward. Munny declines, explaining that he has renounced his past as an outlaw and gunfighter, at the instigation of his wife, now deceased.

But economics motivate him no less than they do the whoremaster of Big Whiskey. After the Kid has gone, Munny gets down in the mud of the pig pen again. Some of his animals have swine fever and he's trying to separate them out. Things are looking desperate.

A short scene follows in which the cowboys return to Big Whiskey to pay the fine of seven horses. One has brought an extra horse for Delilah; as he makes the offer he is framed against a sign which announces 'Meat Market', perhaps an overly obvious commentary on the transaction. But at Alice's insistence the women chase him off, angrily rejecting his attempt to atone for the crime. 'She ain't got no face left, you're going to give her a goddam mangy pony?' There's the merest suggestion of doubt at the rightness of the women's thirst for revenge, in a shot of Delilah looking troubled after the pony has been rejected. Then there's a cut back to Munny, tenderly holding the portrait of his wife. In a gesture heavy with the weight of the Western's traditional polarities, Munny puts down the portrait and picks up his six-shooter. He has changed his mind about the mission; economic imperatives win out over his wife's influence.

Shooting practice

The problem is, has he still got what it takes? A brief sequences discloses that he can no longer shoot straight with a pistol. And he has lost his skill with a horse, as the horse has lost its taste for the saddle. This scene is making a serious dramatic point, that the mission on which Munny is embarking may be too much for him. But it's played for comedy, in the grim-faced determination with which Munny emerges with a shotgun after failing to hit his target with a pistol, the tin can blown away with a resounding crash, and with Munny doing a pratfall as he tries to mount his horse. Eastwood, canny as always, has made a habit out of disarming criticism of his macho image by poking a little fun at himself. In *The Gauntlet* Sondra Locke scores points off him, and in *Every Which Way*

Brittles (John Wayne, left) at the graveside in *She Wore a Yellow Ribbon* (John Ford / Argosy Pictures, RKO Radio Pictures / Universal Pictures, 1949) and (below) Munny at the graveside

But Loose (1978) not only does Locke once again lead him a merry dance, but Clint is upstaged by an orang-utan.

In between the comedy sequences, there's a tender interlude where he visits his wife's grave, taking her flowers; wild flowers, culled from the prairie. Eastwood, something of a student of the Western, cannot be unmindful of the graveside scenes in John Ford's Westerns; John Wayne talking to his dead wife in *She Wore a Yellow Ribbon* (1949), Henry Fonda talking to his dead brother in *My Darling Clementine* (1946).

Comedy or not, though, the emphasis on Eastwood's ageing is inescapable, and marks a watershed in his career. A decade later, *Unforgiven* is still his most recent Western, unless we count *Space Cowboys* (2000), in which the antics of Eastwood's team of elderly astronauts are much more broadly comic. In a recent interview at the National Film Theatre (October 2003) Eastwood indicated that he was unlikely to play a leading role again, and certainly it would be stretching credibility, now he is over seventy, for him to play a hero who can take on the bad guys and dish out the rough stuff. 'We all have it coming, Kid.'

6

There's a consistent pattern to the opening of a Clint Eastwood Western. In *The Outlaw Josey Wales* the hero is a poor southern farmer who is attacked by northern guerrillas during the Civil War. His wife is raped and murdered, his child killed, his farm burned. So Josey, at first seen peacefully ploughing his fields, is turned into an implacable pursuer of his assailants, thirsting for revenge. In *Pale Rider* he is a mysterious preacher, apparently a man of peace, who is persuaded, after witnessing a brutal assault on an unarmed man, to assist a group of miners against a large corporation which is attempting to drive them away. *Unforgiven* goes even further in emphasising the hero's initial unwillingness to get involved in the situation that confronts him. His life has been changed by the love of a good woman; he has left violence behind him. And he's too old anyway.

Of course it's not just Eastwood who has employed this structure. In his book *Sixguns and Society*, Will Wright identifies the hero's reluctance to get involved as a key constituent of the classical Western plot.[8] Thus in several of the series of Westerns he made with Anthony Mann, James Stewart plays a character who prefers not to commit himself; only reluctantly is he drawn into helping those who need him, and usually this is because someone close to him is threatened. Commitment to a cause does not arise from a principled decision to perform his civic duty. In John Ford's films we can observe a similar structure. In *My Darling Clementine* Henry Fonda as Wyatt Earp is offered the job of sheriff of Tombstone, but declines. Only when his brother is killed by the Clanton gang does he pin on the star. In perhaps the most extreme example of this type of story, Ford's *Two Rode Together* (1961), Sheriff Guthrie McCabe (James Stewart) is a cynical and venal lawman who rescues white captives from

Gunned down in (left)
Shane (George Stevens/
Paramount Pictures,
1953) and (below) *Pale
Rider*

75434

the Indians for money. Only right at the end of the picture does he become emotionally involved.

The hero's reluctance to pick up his gun provides tension and drama for the narrative. In terms of motivation there may be several reasons why the hero holds back, but there is always an underlying imperative. As we have seen, violence is necessary to the establishment of civilisation. Savagery and outlawry cannot be defeated by reason and good example alone. Yet the hero must not be seen to relish violence. That would put him on a level with the lawless, with those he must overcome. His anger must be slow to burn, and when it comes to the boil he must have adequate cause. As so often in American cinema, it is the personal rather than the political that is the ultimate motivation. Men fight for families, for sweethearts, for friends, for property, but rarely in the Western for an abstract cause alone. The cause may give legitimacy to their violence, which has a redemptive quality beyond its merely contingent causation, but it is rarely enough to cause the hero to draw his gun.

A classic of the genre in which this narrative pattern is seen most clearly is *Shane*, directed by George Stevens. Shane is a gunman who finds himself drawn towards a community of small farmers terrorised by a big rancher who wants them off their land. At first Shane is aloof, physically distancing himself from the farmers, standing outside the house while they discuss their response to the latest attack. When provoked in the saloon by henchmen of the landowner, he declines to fight. But it becomes clear that unless the farmers physically resist they will be defeated, and at last Shane agrees to help them, having become emotionally involved with one family, Joe Starrett, his wife Marion and their son Joey. Marion abhors violence (she has forbidden Shane to give her son shooting lessons) and implores him not to fight, but Shane knows that only his prowess with a gun can overcome the forces against them. As in *Unforgiven*, Shane is idolised by a younger male (Joey) who is starry-eyed about gunfighting but whom he attempts to persuade that there is no glamour in it. At the end of *Shane*, as in *Unforgiven*, the hero, having killed his man, retreats from the community he has cleansed of evil and withdraws into the obscurity whence he came.

Shane's classic status means that most makers of Westerns would be familiar with it. But Eastwood seems to have internalised this film to a remarkable extent, since not only *Unforgiven* but *Pale Rider* too exhibits many of the same features. In *Pale Rider* the hero is again reluctant to become involved, and is hero-worshipped, this time by a young girl who believes herself in love with him. The similarities have caused some even to describe *Pale Rider* as a remake of *Shane*. Entire sequences from *Shane* find their equivalent, as for example when one of the miners is drawn into a fatal gunfight by the mine owner's hired gunmen, echoing the famous scene in *Shane* when Elisha Cook Jr is gunned down by Jack Palance. And there's a version of the scene in *Shane* when Starrett and Shane work collectively to uproot a huge tree-trunk; in *Pale Rider* it's a boulder which has to be removed.

Thus William Munny's initial refusal of the Kid's invitation to join him in seeking the $1,000 reward is rooted in the conventions of the classic Western, as well as following the pattern of earlier Eastwood movies. Likewise, Munny's reversal of his decision, and in particular the final act of retribution, performed when things get 'personal', is eminently traditional to the genre. It's as well to remember this, since so much of the praise heaped on the film was on account of its challenge to the norm.

7

The Schofield Kid confides in Munny that he's chosen his name from the model of pistol he carries. Wishing to be seen as a man of discrimination, he doubtless intends his choice of weapon to distinguish him from the common run of gunfighters who might carry a Colt. The Smith & Wesson Schofield was manufactured between 1875 and 1878. Most of the 9,000 weapons made went to the US Army, but some found their way into the hands of outlaws, including, apparently, Frank and Jesse James, a fact doubtless known to the Kid (Jesse was at the height of his fame at the time *Unforgiven* begins, and would be shot in the back two years later in 1882).

The Kid is as naive and eager as Munny is grizzled and weary. This figure, of a 'Kid', has many antecedents in the Western. The use of the term

inescapably evokes Billy the Kid, a semi-mythical figure who was shot by Pat
Garrett in July 1881, the very same month as the climactic action of
Unforgiven. There were Kid figures in the Western film from earliest times
(including Howard Hughes's notorious *The Outlaw*, released in 1940), but
in the 1950s a succession of young men peopled the Western who seem to
have been based on the sociological construction of the juvenile delinquent,
callow youths of mean disposition eager to win a reputation as a gunfighter
through a lucky break. The prototype is Skip Homeier in *The Gunfighter*,
who manages to kill Gregory Peck just at the moment when he has decided
to reform and settle down. Homeier played similar parts in a couple of Budd
Boetticher films, *The Tall T* (1956) and *Comanche Station* (1959). Dennis
Hopper was another young actor who made a name playing this kind of part,
as for example in *Gunfight at the OK Corral* (1956).

Young men in the Western are not invariably delinquent, but they
are almost always in need of instruction from their elders and betters. In
The Searchers Jeffrey Hunter as Martin is the butt of a series of heavy-
handed put-downs from Ethan (John Wayne), and in Howard Hawks's
Westerns a succession of youths – Montgomery Clift in *Red River* (1948),
Ricky Nelson in *Rio Bravo* (1959) and James Caan in *El Dorado* (1966) –
are almost crushed by the immense weight of John Wayne's authority.

In *Unforgiven* the Kid will learn a more painful lesson than any of
them. By the end he has stared into the abyss between what he thought he

The Schofield revolver

wanted to be and what he really is, between the spurious glory of gunfighting and its sordid, deadly reality, and has learned a lesson that will keep him alive.

The Kid tempts Will with the $1,000 reward money and tries to elicit outrage with a description of Delilah's injuries ('cut up her face, cut her eyes out, cut her ears off, hell, they even cut her teats'). Writing, as we have seen, is no guarantee of the truth; but oral testimony is equally prone to exaggeration. Will himself embroiders the description still further when he tells his friend Ned that the cowboys also cut her fingers off, 'everything but her cunny, I suppose'. Like so many of the characters in this film, the Kid is caught up in the myth-making process, a victim of his own gullibility, vanity and lust for sensation.

8

Skinny, the proprietor of the brothel (which he hypocritically names a billiard parlour), gets wind of the prostitutes' plan to buy revenge and goes to report to the sheriff. He knows that Daggett will not welcome the trouble caused if gunfighters come to Big Whiskey in search of the reward. Daggett is up on the roof of the house he is building for himself, and bangs his finger with a hammer. His character is an original, or at least an unusual, conception. There's something comic

John Wayne and Montgomery Clift in *Red River* (Howard Hawks / Monterey Productions, United Artists, 1947)

about Daggett, yet no one dares poke fun at him to his face. Hackman's immense weight as a performer suggests the menace that lies just below Daggett's apparently bluff exterior, but in the early scenes he seems no more than another town-taming sheriff employing reasonable force to keep the peace, including the imposition of gun control in his town. Yet the house is, literally, crooked; one of Bill's deputies remarks with a snigger that it 'don't have a straight angle in that whole goddamned porch, or the whole house for that matter'. Little Bill hankers after respectability, constantly railing against 'tramps' and 'loafers', but the community-building spirit with which he sees himself inspired is basically warped.

Skinny reports to Little Bill

Henry Fonda in *My Darling Clementine* (John Ford / Twentieth Century-Fox, 1946)

Like Munny, his eventual nemesis, Daggett is a man with a past who is trying to live it down, and no more than Munny can he lay the demons to rest. At least he has the law on his side, his brutality covered with the fig-leaf of legal authority. Richard Schickel has suggested that in the conception of Daggett, Eastwood was aware of the Rodney King episode in 1991, in which an innocent black man was beaten in full view of a video camera by a phalanx of Los Angeles policemen.[9] The role is thus in part conceived as a comment upon the abuse of authority, and this might suggest another aspect of *Unforgiven*'s novelty, that it works against the stereotype of the upstanding lawman who strides through countless town-taming Westerns, whether played by Errol Flynn in *Dodge City* (1939), by Henry Fonda in *My Darling Clementine* or by Joel McCrea in *Wichita* (1955). Yet though one need not look far to find parallels to Daggett in contemporary actuality, there are plenty of instances in the Western too of corrupt and sadistic lawmen. One of the most memorable is that played by Karl Malden in Marlon Brando's *One-Eyed Jacks* (1960). Significantly he too, like Daggett, is fond of the whip, generally a cowardly weapon in the Western.[10]

(Overleaf) Will and Ned on the trail

9

The scene with Skinny ends on a shot of Daggett looking into the distance, as if already spying the men who will come to his town in search of the reward. Cut to a pasture beside a river, and a homestead: the lyrical music wells up as we hear a cow lowing. A Native American woman looks up from the corn she is tending and sees Munny fording the stream, the sun glinting on the water. The birds are singing, but the woman has a troubled expression. By contrast, her husband Ned's face lights up when he sees Munny. Ned asks his wife, Sally Two Trees, to take care of Munny's horse, but she refuses to greet him as she passes him, and behind the men's backs touches Munny's rifle in apprehension. Like Munny's deceased wife, she is against violence, but she herself has no voice.

Munny's wife, on the other hand, though deceased, is heard from constantly. Munny never ceases to refer to her influence on his life, how she made him renounce whiskey and cussing and killing. Women in the Western are always advising against violence; as Grace Kelly says to Gary Cooper in *High Noon*, 'there's got to be a better way'. In *Stagecoach* (1939) Claire Trevor tries to get John Wayne to escape from the sheriff instead of continuing on to Lordsburg and his fight with the Plummers. Jean Arthur as Marion in *Shane* tries desperately to get her husband and Shane to back off from a confrontation with Ryker, the landowner who is trying to force out the settlers. It's all foreshadowed in Owen Wister's *The*

Cherrilene Cardinal as Sally Two Trees

Female violence: Barbara Stanwyck in *Forty Guns* (Samuel Fuller / Globe Enterprises, 1957)

Virginian, in which the schoolteacher heroine forces the hero to choose between her and standing up to his enemy in a gunfight. There's never any doubt which option he will go for (nor any real doubt that after he has rejected her plea, she will come round).

It's not invariably the case that women are the peacemakers. In *Johnny Guitar* (1954) Mercedes McCambridge and Joan Crawford pick up their guns and fight it out to the end. Barbara Stanwyck is anything but a pacifist in *Forty Guns* (1957), or indeed in any of her Western roles. In *Hannie Caulder* (1971) Raquel Welch plays a woman who learns gunfighting in order to revenge herself on her rapists. If in general women in the Western are against violence, it is not so much because they are inherently 'the gentle sex', nor because in nineteenth-century America they could not plausibly be involved in fighting, but because of what they represent. The civilisation that the hero is fighting for is founded on a certain conception of the family; it is for the women and children that he seeks to 'keep the streets safe'. Civilisation is located in a place of refuge for the defenceless, and this is the realm of women, whose role is essentially a nurturing one. The hero, who often lacks a home himself, recognises that civilisation can only be established by the use of violence. The woman, because of her role, is unable to advocate this necessity, even if she is eventually forced to recognise it.

This is explicit enough in *Unforgiven*. Munny is going against his wife's wishes by once more picking up his gun, but his motivation is clear. He is doing it for his children. To this extent the film is following the tradition of the genre. It may seem that in having the violence instigated by women, by the whores who seek revenge (which is usually the prerogative of men), *Unforgiven* is going against the grain, subverting the genre. But this is not really so. The whores are, by definition of their social role, women who have no families; thus they can function differently from other women. They have chosen (if indeed there ever was a choice) a form of sexual relationship which is conceived as essentially unfamilial, or even anti-familial, because it precludes procreation. For this reason they may advocate and finance the committing of violent acts without disrupting the basic structure of the Western: men = violence/women = peace.

10

Having Munny's closest friend as a black man is an innovatory move. Not that there aren't blacks in the Western. In the 1930s there were even a few B Westerns made specially for black audiences, such as *Harlem Rides the Range* (1939). In the 1960s, as Jim Pines explains, black characters in the Western usually had a more polemical role, as for example in Peckinpah's *Major Dundee* (1964), in which a black soldier becomes the object of racist bigotry by the Confederate soldiers under Dundee's command. Following this, in the 1970s there were a few Westerns in the cycle of 'blaxploitation' films, such as *The Legend of Nigger Charlie* (1972), in which ex-football star Fred Williamson plays a former slave who becomes a gunfighter.[11] More recently, Mario Van Peebles's *Posse* (1993) attempted to rework this mode. What's exceptional about *Unforgiven* is that never once does anyone in the film make reference to Ned's being black (in the original script there is no mention of his colour). Even the brutal Daggett avoids racist abuse.

Ned's wife is Native American, signalled by her name, by the physiognomy of Cherrilene Cardinal, who plays the part, by her hair done up in a pigtail though she wears white clothes, and by her demeanour, archetypical of the noble savage, almost expressionless, but stoical and long-suffering. As with Ned's race, though, nothing is made of it directly.

Will and Ned meet again

Eastwood's films generally display an easy-going, relaxed attitude about racial difference, whether it's Dirty Harry sending up his own supposed prejudice, or Josey's acceptance of Lone Waite, the ageing Cherokee in *The Outlaw Josey Wales*, or in the portrayal of the black community in *Bird* (1988), Eastwood's biography of jazz musician Charlie Parker. There are real gains in being able to cast a black actor in a part which isn't colour-bound, although Michael Carlson wonders whether this 'colour-blindness' may lead to actual social tensions being ignored.[12] Yet perhaps blackness does signify after all, even if no one on screen mentions it. Is it possible we can view a scene of a black man being whipped by a white when Ned is caught by Little Bill without calling to mind the iconography of slavery?

The scene between Will and Ned establishes a number of things. First, just how long it's been since Will fired a shot in anger (eleven years). And it makes clear that, contrary to Will's assertion, it will not be easy killing the two cowboys. Killing was never easy, says Ned, not even when they were young. On the other hand, the two men agree rather glibly, following Will's somewhat spiced-up account of the nature of the cowboys' offence, that they deserve killing. 'I guess they got it coming,' says Ned, a phrase that will be repeated more than once by the end of the film.

Ned reminds Will of what he knows full well, that if his wife was alive he wouldn't be doing this. Will assumes that Ned is refusing to go with him and gets up to leave. But Ned, like Will himself, has allowed himself to be seduced, by the twin dreams of money and adventure. As he stands under his Spencer rifle, fixed to the wall, boasting that he can still hit the eye of a bird, Ned betrays that his liking for domesticity is skin-deep. In a typical Eastwood reaction shot, we see Will, his face in shadow above the eyes, staring intently until a slow smile spreads.

Ned gives a final look at his wife before riding off. A slow track-in shows her standing impassive as the music swells up. She will never see him again. There follows a lyrical passage, a montage of shots of Will and Ned riding through a field of whispering, golden barley, then across a sunset skyline, a sequence mirrored once Ned and Will have caught up with the Schofield Kid; the beauty of nature appears in contrast to the ugly human acts which are to follow.

11

In David Webb Peoples's original script the location of Big Whiskey is placed firmly in 'Nebraska in the Niobrara River country'. This is in the north of the state, up towards the border with South Dakota, doubtless a wild enough area in 1881. Peoples remarks that he chose this setting because it was unusual,[13] but the film shifts the location from Nebraska to Wyoming.

From the early days of the last century, Westerns have used landscape to ensure authenticity. Indeed, in the period before World War I, when American cinema was faced, for the only time in its history, with fierce foreign competition in its domestic market, the Rocky Mountains and the deserts of the southwest gave the American Western film a 'unique selling point' as compared to the Westerns being made in Europe and the eastern United States by the French Pathé company.

Deserts particularly were favoured. Europe too had mountains (and would use them to considerable effect in the Westerns produced in both West and East Germany during the 1960s), but it had no deserts and canyons to rival the spectacular sights of Arizona and Utah (even though Sergio Leone shot his Dollars trilogy in the arid country around Almeria in Spain). Numerous Westerns had their narratives diegetically located on the flat plains of the midwest where were situated the infamous cow-towns of Dodge City, Abiline and Wichita, but the actual scenery of those regions had little to offer the film-maker. Largely featureless, and in any case over-run by fences and corn-fields by the time Hollywood geared up, the landscapes of Kansas and Nebraska were no competition for the splendours further west, and particularly those of the desert southwest.

Eastwood, however, has employed a variety of scenery in the Westerns he has directed. *High Plains Drifter* takes place in a town set on the edge of a lake in dry, rugged country (not the flat plains that the title might suggest). *The Outlaw Josey Wales* moves across the continent, encompassing wooded country in the east, the badlands where Josey meets the Comancheros, and rocky but wooded southwestern scenery where Josey eventually sets up home. *Pale Rider*, mainly shot in Idaho, has mountain scenery very similar to that of *Unforgiven*.[14]

If Nebraska signifies anything in the annals of the west, it's the novels of Willa Cather, but *O Pioneers!* (1913) and *My Ántonia* (1918) dramatise the harsh lives of Scandinavian immigrant farmers on the plains, not the tales of blood and thunder that the Western prefers; the kind of harsh life, indeed, that we see William Munny leading when we first encounter him, in the middle of a flat, featureless waste. Peoples's original choice of location does leave one curious trace behind in the film. When Little Bill first confronts English Bob, the latter says he believed him dead, fallen off his horse while drunk. Bill's reply is: 'Hell, I even thought I was dead, till I found out that it was just I was in Nebraska.' It's a remark which in the original was merely a

Contrasting landscapes

statement of fact but which in the film becomes a surreal non sequitur, reducing Nebraska to bathos.

In contrast to Will, Ned lives in a lush green river-bottom where the corn grows high. The landscape they ride through on their way to Big Whiskey is pretty rather than spectacular. But Big Whiskey itself is set in the high country. Each time we go into the street we see the Rockies spread out all around. Eastwood doesn't linger on their beauty. It's winter time when the three companions arrive, and our primary impression of the landscape is its austerity, even bleakness. Much of the time it is raining. Only in the scene between Will and Delilah after his beating by Little Bill does a lyrical note emerge, when even Will is drawn to comment on the beauty of the snowy scene.

One other location is worth noting. In the harrowing scene when Ned discovers he can't commit murder and Will is forced to take over the shooting of the young cowboy, we're in a deeply eroded, pock-marked landscape, a grim and ugly setting for a grim and ugly deed.

12

Round the camp fire on the trail Will obsessively repeats that he is a reformed man now, that he's just doing the job for money and that it doesn't mean he's going back to the old ways. So insistent is he that Ned is forced to reassure him: 'Well, you ain't like that no more.' 'That's right,' says Will. 'I'm just a fellow now. I ain't no different than anyone else.' This is his delusion; but of course we, the audience, don't believe it.

This quiet scene is rudely interrupted by the whistle of a train. The occupants are discussing the attempted assassination of President Garfield on 2 July 1881. (Shot by Charles J. Guiteau, the President succumbed to his wounds on 19 September.) One of the passengers, who clearly dislikes the English, suspects the assailant must have been a 'John Bull', but a man with his long hair in a pony tail asserts in an impeccably English accent that he was French, on the grounds that the French are known assassins. English Bob, for it is he, offers the opinion that America would be better off with a queen than a president since people would not dare to murder royalty (oblivious,

apparently, to the fact that only a few months previously, in March 1881, Tsar Alexander II had been assassinated in Russia).

Bob's patrician manner is clearly giving offence, and the man who dislikes 'John Bulls' is looking for trouble. The exchange suggests a society in which violence is never very far below the surface, fuelled by xenophobia and boastful posturing. Bob deflects the hostility by proposing they shoot a few pheasants out of the train window, the traditional sport of the English upper classes. Having taken several dollars off his opponents in the competition, thus compounding the insult, he disembarks. On the way from the station Bob develops his provocative analysis of America, calling it savage and uncivilised for its habit of shooting at presidents, ascribing this to extremes of weather and distance, a kind of parody of the geographical determinism of Walter Prescott Webb and others who argued that American exceptionalism derived from the physical characteristics of the continent.[15] Bob's remarks also parody the temptation towards quick and easy explanations of the problem of violence, the problem which the film is setting out to explore.

Bob is an unsavoury character. One of the passengers on the train says that he works for the railroad shooting 'Chinamen' (presumably 'pour encourager les autres'), and as if to confirm this assessment, in the carriage up from the station Bob takes imaginary aim at a couple of Chinese men walking by. After Bob has point-blank challenged the ordinance against carrying weapons, the deputies nervously load their weapons in the sheriff's office. They're scared, but Little Bill Daggett is not, we're told; Daggett has worked in Newton, Hays and Abilene, all tough Kansas cow-towns. In the barber's shop, Bob rambles on about the queen in his highfalutin, bombastic way ('there's a dignity in royalty, a majesty, which precludes the likelihood of assassination') while getting spruced up (being a dandy is just another of his un-American ways). On emerging, muttering something about a cup of tea, he's confronted by the deputies aiming their guns at him. Behind them is Little Bill, the stars and stripes fluttering above his head. It's the Fourth of July, not the best day to go around doing down America. 'Shit and fried eggs,' says Bob, as well he might.

Hollywood has a fondness for making its villains Englishmen and/or casting English actors in such parts, whether it's Anthony Hopkins as Hannibal Lecter in *The Silence of the Lambs* (1990) or Alan Rickman as the terrorist in *Die Hard* (1988) (though ironically Richard Harris was Irish, born in Limerick). Is it that to American ears the English accent always sounds snobbish? Many things can be forgiven more easily than an arrogant assumption of superiority. Certainly Bob is asking for trouble with his contempt for America's egalitarianism.

Bill asks Bob's companion, a mild-mannered bespectacled type, if he too works for the railroad. 'No,' he replies, 'I write.' 'Letters?' inquires Bill. In a semi-literate society, one could presumably make a living writing letters for others, and later Munny will ask the same question. But W. W. Beauchamp is a real writer, presumably the first Bill has encountered, and Bob's biographer.

Thus is introduced one of the film's important themes, the gap between fact and fiction, and the all-pervasive presence and damaging effects of the myth-making tendency. *Unforgiven* offers a study in how reputations may be inflated when the written word gives a spurious authority to a fictionalised account. The dime novel, of course, played a considerable role in the creation of Western mythologies. The first one, *Malaeska: The Indian Wife of the White Hunter*, was published in 1860, and in the remaining years of the century thousands of titles poured forth from the newly invented steam rotary presses, published by the famous firm of

Beadle and Adams and others. Much of this cheap fiction celebrated real people, such as Davy Crockett and Kit Carson, Buffalo Bill and Jesse James, and fictionalised, highly embroidered versions of the lives of the last three appeared while the originals were still alive.

Unforgiven is not the first Western to inscribe a writer into the film itself. In Robert Altman's *Buffalo Bill and the Indians, or Sitting Bull's History Lesson*, the title itself alludes to the typical format of dime novel titles (one of the first and most popular was *Seth Jones, or The Captives of the Frontier*). In the film Burt Lancaster plays Ned Buntline, who in large part created the persona of Buffalo Bill Cody, the fearless frontier scout. In *Cattle Annie and Little Britches* (1980), Lancaster plays outlaw Bill

'Shit and fried eggs'

Burt Lancaster in *Buffalo Bill and the Indians* (Robert Altman / Dino de Laurentiis, Lion's Gate Films, Talent Associates, Norton Simon, 1976

Doolin, who enjoys reading about his exploits in dime novels. And in *The Left-Handed Gun* (1957) Paul Newman as Billy the Kid is intrigued to discover, having just learned to read, that there are books written about him.[16]

13

From Beauchamp's satchel appears an example of his literary efforts. It has a lurid cover characteristic of the dime novel, with a crudely drawn picture of a gunfighter standing amid a crowd of fallen bodies. Its title, *The Duke of Death*, is deliberately misread by Little Bill ('*The Duck of Death*') as a none too subtle insult to Bob. Standing beneath the undertaker's sign, Bob now has to decide whether to resist Bill's order to give up his gun. Bob thinks he has got away with a concealed weapon, but Bill is too smart for him. The savage beating he now administers is, he claims, a warning to anyone else who is thinking of coming to Big Whiskey to claim the reward. But for the audience it's a foretaste of what is to

come, an insight into the viciousness of his character which Ned and Will underestimate at their peril.

What follows is a brief but surprising scene in which Will and Ned ride along discussing sex. Ned is curious whether Will, a widower, goes to whores, but Will replies that Claudia, his wife, wouldn't have wanted that. Ned then asks him if he uses his hand instead. (Is there another Western which brings up the subject of masturbation?) Will's response is that he doesn't miss it that much. This seems to be borne out later, when Will discovers that Ned and the Kid have been taking advances against payment in the form of sex from the whores who are going to pay the reward. When offered a similar arrangement, Will declines, though as we shall see, lack of desire may not be the primary reason.

There's a suggestion of humour in Will's response to Ned's question (he appears, in an unworldly way, to be a little shocked), but the scene touches on something deeper. The association between masculinity and violence is at the heart of the Western. Prowess with a gun and the willingness to use it in the cause of right are the signs of manliness, an association given reinforcement, albeit in parody form, in Little Bill's later tale of Two-Gun Corcoran. Is *Unforgiven* hinting here that once violence is renounced then manliness, indeed the sex drive itself, may be diminished?

The conversation is rudely punctuated by shots fired by the Kid. It's established, in a couple of scenes of wry comedy, that the Kid is chronically short-sighted, a quality that does not sit easily with his bluster about what an experienced killer he is. This is ominous, especially when we return again to Big Whiskey and Little Bill Daggett; Ned, Will and the Kid have no idea just what is in store for them. Little Bill is having some fun with English Bob, repeating his joke about the 'Duck of Death', despite Beauchamp's game insistence that it's the 'Duke', and affecting mock surprise that Bob should have killed seven men in one fight, as the cover of Beauchamp's dime novel appears to suggest. Beauchamp gamely insists that though the cover allows for a little licence, what's inside the book is fact, since it's based on eye-witness accounts.

Little Bill then provides an alternative version of the events in the Bluebottle Saloon in Wichita described in the novel, an account based, he claims, on his own personal observation. Bill asserts that the Duke's opponent, Two-Gun 'Corky' Corcoran, was so named not for packing a brace of six-shooters but for the length of his penis. English Bob's victory over him was the result of a series of farcical accidents, and far from displaying the heroism he shows in Beauchamp's account, Bob was drunk and despatched his opponent while the latter was wounded and unarmed. (Ironically, this will be the exact circumstances of Little Bill's own demise.) Little Bill's story is both a calculated demolition of Western mythology, and, being no less a tall tale than that which it proposes to replace, an example of that very thing. As such Bill's account bears the same relationship to Bob's self-glorifying myth as does *Unforgiven* to the Western itself: it debunks a mythologised west, but ultimately reasserts the mystique of the hero.

We cut now to the camp fire around which Ned, Will and the Kid are bedding down. The Kid, having no biographer, talks up his own exploits, claiming to have killed five men. (It's no surprise when we later learn he has so far killed no one.) He wants to believe that the men he's riding with are similarly heroic, and tries to persuade Ned and Will to boast of their deeds. But, unlike Bob, they refuse. This gives the audience licence to regard them as true heroes. But in so doing are we, the audience, justified in feeling superior to the Kid? Is our need for a hero any less than his?

Back in the jail house Beauchamp, having changed sides, has been allowed out and sits with pen and paper recording Little Bill's every word, complicit even to the point now of echoing Bill's little joke about the Duck of Death. Beauchamp's fascination with violence comes uncomfortably close to that of the film audience itself. Indeed, one might even see his keenness to describe and analyse the exploits of killers as a sort of mischievous parody of academic scholars of the genre, relishing at second-hand in the safety of their studies a world so different from their own.

Little Bill now gives a demonstration to Beauchamp of just how hard it is to kill a man. It's a lesson which Munny in his different style later seeks to impress on the Kid. Fundamentally, it's a point about different kinds of character. Some can do it, some can't. Little Bill and Munny have this in common, that they know no fear. By contrast, the Kid is all bluster, and Beauchamp can barely bring himself to touch the gun which Little Bill thrusts at him. Nor does Bob take the gun when it is offered to him. Bob can kill those weaker than him, but he's afraid to take on Little Bill.

It's one of the grand themes of the Western, that manhood is about having the courage to kill if necessary. What *Unforgiven* does is to dig deeper into the question of just what sort of manhood this is, what sort of people are willing to undertake the task. In the classic Western the hero always has a bit of the wilderness in him. In *Unforgiven* the savagery is more pronounced; less easily 'forgiven'.

Bob's gun is returned

The storm that rolled around the camp fire in the last scene but one has now broken, the heavens opening on Ned, Will and the Kid as they ride along. Meanwhile, back at Big Whiskey Bob is being run out of town. He asks for his gun back and Little Bill hands it to him with the barrel bent over. There could be no more graphic comment on the link between prowess with a gun and masculinity. As the carriage conveys him through town to the train station, Bob unleashes a torrent of abuse ('a plague on the whole stinkin' lot of you'). It's a clever touch, perhaps not obvious to an American audience unfamiliar with the relation between class and speech in England, that Bob's accent, formerly so plummy when he discoursed on the sacred aura of the queen, has reverted to a broad and common cockney. Bob has in reality no more social status than the unpolished Americans he despises.[17]

Back in Little Bill's house, with its ill-constructed, leaky roof, Little Bill is warming to the task of recounting his exploits to Beauchamp. He speaks with deliberate slowness so that Beauchamp can get down every word: 'I do not like assassins. Men of low character.' He's becoming self-important now he's got a biographer, and eager to expatiate on his distinction between the respectable and the disreputable. In Greely's saloon Ned and the Kid are upstairs with the whores. Will refuses to join them. He has a fever and is starting to hallucinate, seeing the faces of his victims. As the thunder rumbles, Little Bill enters. His confrontation with

A beating in *High Plains Drifter* (Clint Eastwood / Malpaso, Universal Pictures / Columbia Trista Home Video, 1972). (Overleaf) Munny tended by Delilah

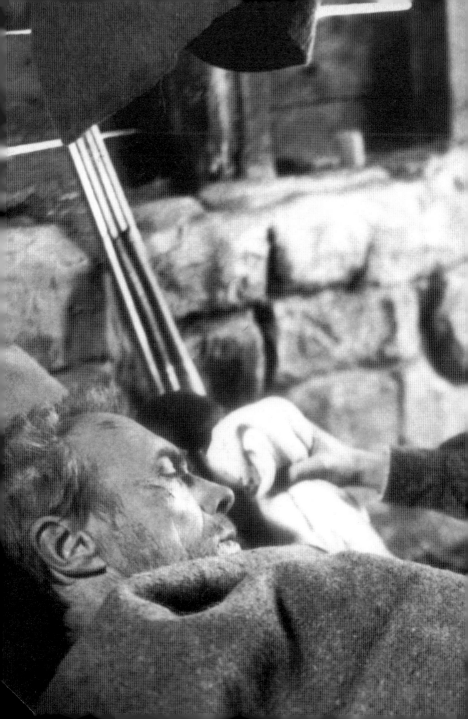

Will follows the same course as that with English Bob. Initially he invites him to give up his weapon, knowing he is armed and will refuse; then Little Bob can 'legitimately' beat him to a pulp for resisting. There's a chilling sadism in the long drawn-out process of interrogation, and a self-righteous hypocrisy in the mask of legality Little Bob gives to his beatings.[18]

It's not the first time Eastwood is beaten to a frazzle in his Westerns. In a flashback in *High Plains Drifter* he is set upon by a gang of men. In *The Outlaw Josey Wales* he's beaten senseless at the beginning of the film, and he receives several beatings in his Italian Westerns. Perhaps only James Stewart in his series of films with Anthony Mann gets beaten up more regularly out west. By contrast it's hard to recall a scene in which John Wayne is beaten into submission. (Eastwood once remarked that in his films he did all the things John Wayne wouldn't do.) In the Western some heroes are ennobled by suffering; having plumbed the depths, they rise above them, and perhaps these are the heroes the modern sensibility most responds to. It's another indication of how Eastwood is in touch with the contemporary *Zeitgeist*.

14

Ned and the Kid meet up with Will outside town, having jumped out of the upstairs window of the saloon to avoid Little Bill. Despite this ignoble

'I wouldn't normally pay no notice to high country like this'

retreat, the Kid is still full of bluster, alternately talking up Will's heroism, trying to find a reason why he didn't fight ('his pistol must have jammed'), and contemptuously dismissive ('he ain't nothing but a broken-down pig farmer'). Suffering from fever and his wounds, Will endures a dark night of the soul. 'I've seen the angel of death … he's got snake eyes … I'm scared of dying … I seen Claudia too – her face was all covered with worms.' Without the fear of death, there can be no true heroism.

In the morning the torrential rain which had accompanied the encounter with Little Bill has turned to snow, apparently an unlooked-for occurrence at the Canadian location for the Big Whiskey set, but it makes for a pretty scene, as Will remarks, looking out over a stunning snowscape of distant mountains: 'I wouldn't normally pay no notice to high country like this, trees, but I sure notice 'em now.'[19] It's his first meeting with Delilah, the scarred prostitute, a delicate piece of writing and handled wonderfully well by the actors. She informs him Ned and the Kid have been getting sexual favours as an advance against payment for killing the two cowboys, and offers Will a 'free one' too. He gives her a look, part surprised, part bashful, and declines. She assumes it's because of her disfigurement, and gets up from her position beside him to move forward towards the camera, so that her face is hidden from him, though not from the audience. She tries to cover the hurt of rejection by pretending that she has not been offering herself, that he could get the free one not from

Delilah puts on her bonnet

her but from the other whores, but in a gesture that reveals more than she knows she obscures her face by putting on her bonnet. Will, mortified to have offended her, however unwittingly, tries to retrieve the situation, explaining that it's only because of his wife that he has declined. Delilah's face is in close-up, screen left, while Will is further back to the right. We watch her as she listens, wanting to believe him, hardly daring to.

The tenderness of this scene is matched by the delicacy of the next. It's a scene about killing which contains in miniature the theme of the film. Will, Ned and the Kid lie in wait to ambush one of the cowboys they have been hired to kill. Ned takes a shot at him with his Spencer carbine but succeeds only in bringing down his horse, which breaks the cowboy's leg. Ned cannot bring himself to finish him off. Faced with a sitting duck, he freezes, his face overcome with shame and something more profound. Will takes the gun and carefully aims. After several shots he gets the cowboy in the gut. The Kid, who cannot see that far, continually demands to be told what's happening. 'Do you think we killed him?' Will stares at him, his face resigned, almost weary. 'Yeah, we killed him. I guess.' While the Kid shouts abuse at the stricken cowboy, who is crying out piteously, Will calls down to the boy's companions to give him a drink. As another cowboy shouts up at them that his friend is dying, Will stares expressionless at the ground, absent-mindedly picking at the rocks. The script gives no more than the few bare lines of dialogue. All the meaning is in the actors' exchanges of looks, Ned appalled by what they have done, in a state of shock, Will grim-faced, feeling the awful burden of his actions.[20]

Soon after Ned announces he's had enough and is going home. Little Bill organises a search party to pursue the killers of the cowboy. Before the posse ride off they throw a brick through the whores' window. Delilah is disturbed by how things have turned out and the fact that one of the cowboys is dead. 'I didn't think they'd really do it.' But Strawberry Alice, always the ring-leader, shouts out at the mob: 'He had it coming for what he done', a phrase that has increasing resonance each time it is uttered. Then Ned is brought in. Little Bill has W. W. Beauchamp in tow, and, clearly enjoying performing a role, is now talking in the stilted cadence of a character from a dime novel as he demands the names of

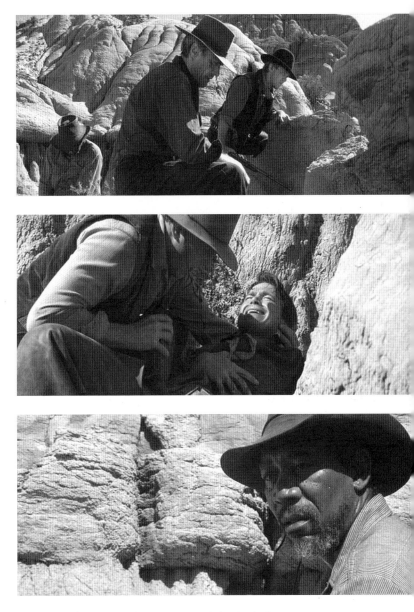

Aftermath of a shooting. (Overleaf) 'not gentle like before, but bad'

Ned's 'villainous friends … I'll be glad to hear the names and whereabouts of those murderous sons of bitches.'

Meanwhile back at the ranch where the other cowboy is hiding, the Kid anxiously enquires whether Will wants to shoot the cowboy himself. 'You can shoot him,' Will snaps, exasperated. Cut back to Ned, stripped to the waist and tied to the bars of the jail as Little Bill whips him ferociously. The onlookers, including W. W. Beauchamp, appear shame-faced; there's a good deal of looking away in this film, whether from shame or revulsion, and the camera tracks round town observing the faces of the whores, now that the full effects of their action are starting to unravel.

Beauchamp, the dutiful scribe, has now put his writing skills at the service of a torturer, noting the discrepancies in the story that Ned has given under duress. In one of the most chilling moments in the film, Little Bill announces, in a voice low with menace, that the whores will be sent for to give the names they have been told. 'Them whores are going to tell different lies than you, and when their lies ain't the same as your lies, well, I ain't gonna hurt no woman, but I'm gonna hurt you, and not gentle like before, but bad.'

Cut back again to the ranch. The second cowboy is the one who actually cut up Delilah, and whereas the first cowboy to be killed was relatively innocent and fair of features, making his assassination by Will a cold-blooded murder, the second cowboy is thick-set and coarse in his

Beauchamp looks away

speech. As a companion remarks, 'A man ain't polite he oughta get shot.' Like history when it repeats itself, the first killing is a kind of tragedy, but the second has elements of farce, the man being shot as he sits in the shithouse by the Kid, then Will once more struggling to mount his horse as the Kid blasts away blindly at assailants he can't even see.

15

Now follows the greatest scene in the film, perhaps the best thing Eastwood ever did. On the windswept prairie outside Big Whiskey, Will and the Kid wait, Will standing beside a solitary tree, the Kid seated beneath. The Kid, clearly in a state of shock, talks and talks while sipping from a whiskey bottle, blustering about the killing. He admits to being scared 'a little', but boasts of his deed: 'I blazed away.' In a belated moment of candour he admits this is his first killing, but is still trying to talk up his bravery: 'I killed the hell of him, didn't I? Three shots, and he was taking a shit …' his voice cracks up. 'Take a drink, Kid,' says Will, reading the situation but too delicate in his feelings to want to embarrass the poor boy.

The Kid can no longer hide his trauma. 'It don't seem real, how he ain't gonna never breathe again, ever …' Munny has been staring grimly into the distance, absorbing the Kid's pain, and now responds, speaking slowly, as if to himself: 'It's a hell of a thing, killing a man. You take away

Elements of farce

After the killings: Will and the Kid

all he's got and all he's ever gonna have.' Like all the best Western actors, Eastwood creates his effect with the minimum of melodramatics, articulating the words calmly, slowly, with dignity. Never has Eastwood seemed closer, in appearance and spirit, to such great Western actors of the past as William S. Hart and Randolph Scott.

Summoning up the last of his bravado, the Kid seeks justification, repeating what Alice had shouted through the window, and Ned before her: 'Well, I guess he had it coming.' Will's reply has all the lapidary terseness of the classical Western hero, articulating the deep stoicism that is the last resort of the loner: 'We all have it coming, Kid.' Never was a truer word spoken in a Western, facing up

Will takes the Schofield

to the inescapable fact of death, which lies in wait for us all, both the good and the bad. As far as death is concerned, there are no just deserts; as Munny will later articulate to the dying Little Bill, 'Deserve's got nothing to do with it.'

Confirmation of this bleak philosophy comes immediately. One of the girls from Greely's rides up with their payment for the killings and Munny learns to his horror that Little Bill has tortured Ned to death; Ned, the only one of the three who did not commit a killing, and who, in revulsion at the very idea, has abandoned the mission to ride home. As he learns the details of Ned's last moments, Munny picks up the bottle and almost absent-mindedly begins to drink. With icy determination he demands the Kid hand him his Schofield revolver, an act redolent with all the significance that the Western genre can impart. The Kid gives it up readily: 'I don't kill nobody no more.'

16

We now move to the last act, one that appears to overturn everything that the film has been working towards. Up to this point, the film has been developing a critique of the function of violence in the cinema and of the way that violence is portrayed. At every opportunity Munny himself has avowed his conversion to a peaceable life by his late wife, his renunciation of his former role of killer. Though he has by now been involved in the killing of two men, he has embarked on the mission only in desperation, in dire need of money. For his part, Ned has found that he can no longer, if he ever could, shoot a man he doesn't even know in cold blood. The Kid, full of bluster, has discovered the real nature of murder, has been traumatised by his assassination of a man caught literally with his trousers down. Even the whores seem taken aback by what their desire for vengeance has unleashed.

But now Munny himself is fired by that self-same lust for vengeance, fuelled by the unaccustomed drink of whiskey. He turns before our very eyes into the cold-blooded killing machine he once was. As the thunder rumbles he rides through the black night and sheeting rain towards the lights of Greely's saloon, past the body of his

friend, lit by a hellish light and adorned with a sign: 'this is what happens to assassins around here'.

Inside, Little Bill is pleased with himself, strutting around, confidently giving out orders for the morrow when his posse will hunt down William Munny. 'We're bound to come across somebody that seen these – skunks.' Just before he utters the last word he hears the sound of a gun being cocked. He turns and sees Munny at the door with a shotgun. Munny asks who owns 'this shithole'. Skinny comes forward; appropriately, for one who has shown himself so much more concerned with property than people, his last words are of money, volunteering that he bought the saloon for $1,000, exactly the price his whores have offered for revenge. Munny's response is shocking. Without warning, he blasts the whoremaster with his shotgun.

It's shocking because we have spent the entire movie hearing Munny say he doesn't do this sort of thing any more. It's shocking because it's without warning, indeed without explanation before the event. And it's shocking because Skinny is unarmed and is not in fact guilty of killing Ned. But of course a movie is not a courtroom trial. Skinny is morally culpable if not legally, for being an accessory. And he is without doubt the least attractive character in the movie. In Anthony James's excellent performance he comes across as unctuously subservient to those in power such as Little Bill, while a heartless bully to the whores whose lives he controls. James's

'this is what happens to assassins around here'

'Well, sir, you are a cowardly son of a bitch': Skinny and Bill meet their nemesis

face, eyes set close together, cheeks hollow, with a thin, straggly beard, give him a head start in portraying a mean-minded exploiter of the weak.

Are these reasons enough to get him blown away? Little Bill doesn't think so. 'Well, sir, you are a cowardly son of a bitch.' Bill has a lively sense of morality except where his own actions are concerned. 'You just shot an unarmed man ... You'd be William Munny out of Missouri, killed women and children.' There's an obvious irony in this charge, given that Munny has come to avenge the women Little Bill has refused justice. But Munny is in no mood now to debate ethics. 'I've killed just about everything that walks or crawled at one time or another, and I'm here to kill you, Little Bill, for what you did to Ned.' It's not justice now, it's personal.

'Deserve's got nothing to do with it'

Little Bill remains defiant, but as we cut from one face to another around his associates, we see the fear on their faces. No one wants to stick their neck out. As Munny's shotgun misfires, Little Bill's eye twitches. He too feels the strain, but has the nerve to go for his gun. He then receives a practical demonstration of the lesson in shooting he had given with such smug self-satisfaction to W. W. Beauchamp earlier. While all around him shoot their guns in a frenzy, Munny draws and fires his Schofield with deadly precision, downing five men, including Little Bill. One of them, Bill's fat deputy, Munny shoots in the back as he tries to run away. We have left the chivalry of the gunfight well behind now, though Munny allows non-combatants to leave.

W. W. Beauchamp emerges, terrified, from under a dead body, but soon remembers his calling and starts making mental notes about what he's seen. It's important, he thinks, who Munny shot first: 'When confronted by superior numbers, an experienced gunfighter will always fire on the best shot first,' he says, as if quoting from one of his own works. But Munny doesn't go by the book. 'I was lucky in the order …' (i.e. it was chance he got Little Bill first). Beauchamp departs. Little Bill proves not quite dead. 'I don't deserve this … I was building a house,' he gasps as he lies bleeding on the floor. This is a delicious non sequitur, but in any case Munny rejects Little Bill's plea for justice, as Little Bill had rejected others'. 'Deserve's got nothing to do with it,' he says as he delivers the *coup de grace*.

17

Two of Eastwood's co-stars, Morgan Freeman and Gene Hackman, have testified that the director intended *Unforgiven* to have a message, or at least a moral. In the documentary that accompanies the film in the DVD Special Edition, *All on Accounta Pullin' a Trigger*, Freeman says the moral is anti-violence: 'Nothing good comes of it ultimately. It does damage the soul.' Hackman concurs: 'I like to believe that he set out to make an anti-violence pro-woman picture.' Eastwood himself is happy to go along with this idea: 'I'm not doing penance for all the characters in action films I've portrayed up till now. But I've reached a stage of my life, and we've reached a stage of our history where I said to myself that violence shouldn't be a source of humor or attraction … We had a chance here to deal with the moral implications of violence.'[21] The writer of the script, David Webb Peoples, is more circumspect, but does try to draw a distinction between *Unforgiven* and earlier films: 'There's certainly no intention on my part to write an anti-violence picture. On the other hand, I think violence is horrifying and I think the reason people think this is an anti-violent picture is that so many other pictures are at least intellectually pro-violence, in other words they suggest if the good guy just beats up the bad guy this will make everything better, and I don't think life's like that, I don't think it's ever as simple as that, I think it's really hard to figure out who the good guy is and who the bad guy is to begin with. There is an ambiguity to it, from each person's perspective the other guy might be the bad guy, so it's not so much anti-violence as recognising that violence is frightening.'

Such an interpretation can be sustained at least up until the moment when Munny enters Greely's saloon for the last time. The initial burst of violence which sets the whole story off, the slashing of Delilah's face, is an act of brutality which both has long-term effects on many people, and whose human consequences are visible on the unfortunate girl's face for the remainder of the film. Munny is shown to be a reformed character who has renounced violence, at least by his own account, and who is persuaded to embark on his enterprise of vengeance only because of his dire need of money. The killing of the first cowboy is drawn-out, messy and traumatising for Ned, who then abandons the mission. The second killing, of the man in the outhouse, is part farce but its aftermath is telling. The Kid affects bravado but can't sustain it as the realisation of what he has done comes upon him, reducing him to tears. So shocked is the Kid that he renounces gunplay forthwith, and even Munny appears suitably chastened by the experience. As he remarks, 'It's a hell of a thing, killing a man.'

It's possible to argue that even the final shoot-out is consistent with the rest of the film, if we believe that the audience feels equivocal about William Munny. After all, Munny is killing not out of principle but from personal motives, and is none too fussy about how he does it. He shoots an unarmed man (Skinny), shoots another, one of Bill's deputies, in the back, and he kills Little Bill while he is lying on the floor wounded. Killing is an ugly business, we can see, and as Munny himself says, has little to do with justice. Some of those involved in making the film have maintained that between Munny and Little Bill the film is even-handed. Eastwood says that Little Bill has 'a point of view', and the scriptwriter David Webb Peoples remarks, 'I liked Little Bill a lot.'[22] But if notionally Little Bill can be seen as a sheriff trying only a little too enthusiastically to keep the peace, the relish with which he goes about delivering his 'justice' surely does not recommend him as a model lawmaker. And despite Munny's disavowal, it is hard not to feel that Little Bill does indeed deserve what he gets, his final cold-blooded despatch having been prepared by his callous treatment of the whores at the beginning, by his brutal treatment of English Bob (even though Bob had also in a sense 'deserved it') and finally by his sadistic murder of Ned. And if there were any doubt, the casting of Gene Hackman, while it gives the character great dramatic weight, tips the scales decisively. In a competition with Eastwood for the audience's sympathies there can only be one winner.[23]

What does the audience feel as Munny goes back into Greely's? Munny's motivation is no longer justice for a wronged woman, or even money to support his children, but revenge against the man who has killed his friend. If it's really an anti-violence picture, we ought at this point feel that Munny is letting himself down, and that the final bout of killing is a betrayal of his wife's legacy. In fact, it's almost impossible to respond to the film in that way. We do not view him dispassionately through the prism of our awakened feelings of anti-violence. Instead, we are on his side, cheering as single-handed he takes on a whole saloon full of opponents and routs them. Does this suggest we have never really been convinced by Munny's reformation? Though we don't doubt the sincerity of the character's renunciation of his past, our knowledge of the Eastwood persona derived from other Westerns causes us to suspend our belief. And though we see his unsteady aim and his loss of horsemanship, nevertheless the way Eastwood is presented on screen, the frequent menacing stares from under the brim of his hat that are such a trademark, indicate that the capacity for violence is merely held in check, not renounced for ever. And so we are not surprised, indeed are even gratified, that having worked against the founding myth of the Western for most of its length, that strong and just men must use violence to impose order and civilisation, in the last reel *Unforgiven* reverts to tradition. If ever a film had its cake and ate it too, surely this is it.

18

Munny calls to the cowed citizenry not to shoot at him when he comes out of the saloon or he will wreak a terrible revenge on them too. After enjoining them to bury Ned, he rides slowly through the rain into the night, the women of Greely's standing in the street to watch him go.

The whole of this last sequence before the coda is played almost exactly as written in the 1984 version of David Webb Peoples's script. Peoples originally wrote it in 1975, when it was titled 'The Cut-Whore Killings'. It was optioned in 1984 by Francis Ford Coppola, who retitled it 'The William Munny Killings'. (Peoples remarked[24] that his original title was great if you've seen the movie, but otherwise, perhaps, obscure.) Eastwood then optioned the script in 1985 and sat on it for several years. The eventual title, *Unforgiven*, was Eastwood's idea, who made the change just before shooting started. Peoples says he was happy with this, indeed couldn't think of a better. 'It has a lot of implications without saying anything definite.'

It's a testament to the excellence of the writing that so very little was altered between script and screen. Even so, Peoples remarks that 'it blew my mind' that so little was changed, his experience of the movie industry having led him to expect sweeping transformations. In this last scene the only notable change is that the language is toned down somewhat, as it is throughout the film, presumably to secure a more lenient MPAA rating.[25] Thus, instead of 'I'm comin' outta here an' any fucker I see out there, I'm gonna kill him' the film has: 'Any man I see out there, I'm gonna kill him.'

There is a change in the next scene, however, for the script has Munny returning to his two children. The boy, Will, shows him the money which the Kid has left as he passed through, and asks his father if he had to kill anyone to get it.

MUNNY (it's an effort): Naw, son, I didn't kill nobody.

It's one of the few places where the film significantly diverges from the script, and as so often Eastwood's instincts are good, since this scene of Munny's return to his children tells us nothing new, merely adding a mawkish note.[26]

According to Eastwood's biographer Patrick McGilligan, Peoples never even met Eastwood until the film was shot and edited.[27] Eastwood isn't himself a writer, but rather a director who is always looking for a good script and who, when he gets one, is inclined to go with it. Many of the things one might imagine as directorial touches were there from the start, such as the business of Munny shooting tin cans off the fence with a shotgun, or his difficulties with his horse, or even W. W. Beauchamp wetting himself when confronted by Little Bill. Munny himself no longer has only three fingers on his left hand as the script says (a detail that would have added little to our sense of his lurid past and would have been a nuisance to the actor). Another change is that the script specifies that Munny is thirty-five to forty years old. Eastwood was in fact over sixty when he played the part, and it has been suggested that the star held on to the script until he thought he was old enough for the role; if so, it was evidently his idea, not the writer's, to play Munny as middle-aged.[28]

Apart from such minor alterations as substituting pheasants for the turkeys specified by the script in the shooting competition scene on the train, most of the changes are simply reductions in the length of scenes, cutting out extraneous dialogue, as with this excised exchange among the cowboys out at the ranch guarding their friend 'Quick Mike' and making fun of his plight. 'See anything out there, Buck?'

BUCK: Hell, yes I did, seen about two hundred fellers packin' rifles ... Fuckers got the place surrounded, says they want Quick Mike's ass ... I says "How much?" They says "About five." I says "Dollars?" They says "Cents." I says, "Sold."

19

Though Eastwood is unusually faithful to the script, he brings to the composition of the visual image his own highly distinctive style. As a director Eastwood has always had a liking for the crepuscular, for scenes shot in semi-darkness with just one or two sources of light. Some of the interiors of *Pale Rider* are shot with so little illumination that only the silhouettes of the characters are visible. Eastwood's director of photography on that film was Bruce Surtees, popularly known as 'The Prince of Darkness' because of his fondness for working with a low level of light. Camera operator on *Pale Rider* was Jack Green, who by the 1990s had graduated to becoming Eastwood's preferred director of photography. Green, obviously with Eastwood's backing, continued with this distinctive style on *Unforgiven*, a style which Eastwood's biographer Patrick McGilligan rather snidely relates to the star's well-known preference for shooting his pictures quickly, and therefore economically:

The 'Prince of Darkness' aesthetic, which grew to be recognized as the house style, was sometimes striking, sometimes pushed to extremes. Clint resisted bright or 'fill-in' lighting; it took time and money, and anyway he preferred scenes shadowed with darkness. It became another component of his 'shoot-the-rehearsal' philosophy of supposed spontaneity and realism. If the low lighting didn't flatter some of the leading ladies, well, the cinematographers understood that, at least, the boss benefited from the shadows that concealed his accumulating age lines.[29]

Far from being an admirable trait which more Hollywood film-makers might emulate in an era of reckless spending, Eastwood's keenness to save money is held against him by McGilligan, as evidence of his personal meanness. (On the other hand, David Thomson in *The New Biographical Dictionary of Film* prefers to describe Eastwood as 'a model of managerial economy'.)[30] In fact, Richard Schickel, who was present for much of the filming of *Unforgiven*, found Eastwood exercising a more painstaking approach this time round, showing 'a willingness to rehearse a little longer than usual, make more takes, do more coverage of complex scenes'.[31] McGilligan's implication that low-key lighting was in part designed to flatter the director/star at the expense of his fellow actors seems a little churlish, too. It would be hard to recall a film in which a major star directs himself which is less concerned to show off his physical appeal. Eastwood wallowing in the mud with pigs or recovering from a beating is hardly a pretty picture, and in close-ups the lines on his face are there for all to see.

Unforgiven, though, is dark even by the standards of previous Eastwood works. The action of the film begins and ends at night in Greely's saloon and whorehouse, the interiors dimly lit and shadowy. One can read this as 'realism'; on the nineteenth-century frontier, bright lights were the exception. More symbolically, one may note that night is the time when we see into the darkness of Munny's soul. Round the camp fire on the open plains, when he recalls his earlier, bloody life, at Greely's when he is beaten by Little Bill, at the end when his desire for vengeance brings to the surface his murderous instincts.

Yet even daytime scenes are often darkly lit. When the Kid outlines to Munny the deal awaiting in Big Whiskey, they sit inside Munny's house. It's not a studio set but an actual building, though doubtless constructed solely for the purpose of filming.[32] In this scene, the light appears to come only from the door and windows; there is no obvious source of light inside the room. Often, as they move about,

A frame within a frame within a frame

the characters are visible only in outline against the open door, and sometimes scarcely visible at all. In one shot Munny stands in the doorway, his back to the main source of light, with only the bottom left-hand quarter of his face visible, up as far as the eye. So we have a frame (of part of his face) within a frame (the open doorway) within the frame of the film itself. It's a dramatic composition, which whether economical or not is aesthetically effective, spare, elegant, focusing our gaze onto Munny's response. Whether the viewer feels such a lighting style is art or mere artiness is perhaps ultimately a matter of taste.

Response is one of the things Eastwood is good at. It's often said that this is the true test of a great screen actor, that he can command the frame even when not talking, even when apparently doing nothing. Sergio Leone remarked that Eastwood came across as lazy, like a cat, or like a snake only uncoiling himself when the director shouted 'Action!' Perhaps Leone's most revealing remark was this:

The story is told that when Michelangelo was asked what he had seen in one particular block of marble, which he chose among hundreds of others, he replied that he saw Moses. I would offer the same answer to the question why did I choose Clint Eastwood, only backwards. When they ask me what I saw in Clint Eastwood ... I reply that what I saw, simply, was a block of marble. And that was what I wanted.[33]

The Eastwood stare

In other words, it is Clint's stillness, his ability to do nothing but just be, which helps give him presence. One of the most effective parts of his repertoire is the stare. Sometimes it's hostile, as with his terrifying glare at Little Bill as he enters the saloon for the final confrontation, at other times quizzical, as in his look at Delilah when she appears to offer him a 'free one'; at others stoical as when, after they have killed the second cowboy, the Kid cracks up and Will looks out towards the horizon. And often when we get this look, the framing gives it emphasis by obscuring the upper part of Eastwood's face with a hat, just the eyes peering out from under the brim.

20

Some years later, Mrs Ansonia Feathers made the arduous journey to Hodgeman County to visit the last resting place of her only daughter.

William Munny had long since disappeared with the children … some said to San Francisco where it was rumored he prospered in dry goods.[34]

And there was nothing on the marker to explain to Mrs Feathers why her only daughter had married a known thief and murderer, a man of notoriously vicious and intemperate disposition.

As this text scrolls up the screen before the closing titles, we hear for one last time the plangent tune, called 'Claudia's Theme', which Eastwood himself composed uncredited. His interest in music goes back a long way. As a young man he made himself into a passable piano player and in 1959, while starring in *Rawhide*, he'd even issued an album of Western songs called *Cowboy Favorites*. In 1969 he'd appeared singing on screen in the musical Western *Paint Your Wagon*. He has a long-standing interest in jazz, which led among other things to his film biography of Charlie Parker, *Bird*, and in 1982 he played a country and western singer in *Honkytonk Man*.

Unforgiven is book-ended by long shots of a sunset. In the first a man is digging a grave; a shack and a tree are outlined against the sky. In the second a line of washing has been strung out by the shack (the symbolism of which is perhaps easily enough read). A lone figure walks towards a headstone, removes his hat and stands in reverence, before a dissolve removes him from the image. (This sunset shot appears in one other place in the film, though reversed left to right, just before we catch our first glimpse of Munny, in the pig pen. So although the scene with the pigs sets out to create a decidedly unheroic image, there's nevertheless a quick reminder of another dimension to Munny's persona.)

The sunset is a beautiful image with which to end the film, richly evocative, wistful, peaceful after the brutality of the last few scenes. Yet isn't it a little too pat? Munny has been protesting throughout the film that he has reformed, thanks to the influence of his 'dear, departed' wife. What we have just witnessed makes it clear his reform was only skin-deep. How can he honestly stand at her grave, head bowed, as if he still acknowledges his wife as his spiritual guide? One more example, perhaps, of how the movie wants it both ways, wants to show you that Munny's wildness still churns beneath his placid exterior, and wants you to think he's finally found inner peace.

Right at the end of the credits, after most of the audience have probably departed, comes Eastwood's discreet dedication of the film, to 'Sergio and Don'. By this point in his career Eastwood had come to appreciate the interest taken in his work by European critics. 'Especially here in France, there are those you call "cinephiles" – is that the word? – who are interested in movies not only as an entertaining spectacle to eat popcorn by. Now the rest of the world is beginning to come to an agreement around this way of thinking.'[35] And so the reference to his two mentors could be a knowing one, using first names only, because the cinephiles, those who truly value his work, would know that these referred to Don Siegel and Sergio Leone.

In a sense 'Sergio and Don' are the two poles of Eastwood's oeuvre. Don Siegel, who directed Eastwood in five films, including his first great hit, *Dirty Harry*, represents Eastwood's roots in classical American cinema, a cinema of craftsmanship, economical, spare, all the parts in harmony, everything subordinated to the story. Sergio Leone, who directed Eastwood in the so-called 'Dollars trilogy' of *A Fistful of Dollars*, *For a Few Dollars More* and *The Good, the Bad and the Ugly*, is

The last sunset. Eastwood in *Per un pugno di dollari* / *A Fistful of Dollars* (Sergio Leone / Jolly Film, Constantin Film, Ocean Films / MGM Home Entertainment, 1964) and *Dirty Harry* (Don Siegel / Warner Bros., Malpaso / Warner Home Video, 1971)

Eastwood and Don Siegel during filming of *Two Mules for Sister Sara* (Don Siegel / Universal Pictures, Malpaso, 1970)

the flamboyant embroiderer of the classical Western, concocting baroque embellishments which depart radically from the American origins of the genre. Eastwood is the heir of both, his roots in the traditional forms of the genre but alert to shifts in public taste that require a more adventuresome approach.

Or is it quite so simple? Several of Siegel's Westerns are themselves departures from the pure form. *Two Mules for Sister Sara*, is, perhaps, the Western as a site for the battle of the sexes; *The Beguiled* a gothic melodrama in which the Eastwood hero loses such a battle; *The Shootist*, an elegiac coda to the genre, full of nostalgia and regret. Whereas Leone's Westerns with Eastwood, despite the undeniable extravagance of their style, are narratively pared down almost to the bone, simple tales of revenge divested of the ideological complexities of manifest destiny or 'the Indian problem'. *Unforgiven* would undoubtedly have appealed to both Eastwood's mentors, if for different reasons.

21

Unforgiven proved to be a triumph for Eastwood. Critically the film received his best notices for years, perhaps his best ever. *Hollywood Reporter* called it 'a magnificently realized work'. *Variety* said it was 'a classic Western for the ages … a tense, hard-edged, superbly dramatic yarn that is also an exceedingly intelligent meditation on the West … a mature, contemplative film, with all that implies for b.o. prospects'. Vincent Canby in the *New York Times* called it 'a most entertaining Western' and considered this Eastwood's 'richest, most satisfying performance'.[36] If *Variety*'s intention was to warn that the film might be too good for the box office, the director/star need not have worried. *Unforgiven* went on to gross over $100 million in the US market and a further $58 million in the rest of the world. Of Eastwood's films only *Every Which Way But Loose* and *In the Line of Fire* have ever done better business, and *Unforgiven*'s take is three times the average gross for an Eastwood picture.

The film's performance at the box office was undoubtedly helped by its great success at the Academy Awards that year. *Unforgiven* won no less than four Oscars: to Joel Cox for Editing, to Gene Hackman for Best Supporting Actor, to Eastwood for Best Director, and to Eastwood again, as producer, for Best Picture. For sixty years, no Western had won the award for Best Picture, since *Cimarron* in 1930. Undoubtedly there was a feeling that Westerns lacked the prestige required to win a major prize. Then Kevin Costner's high-minded Western epic *Dances With Wolves* won in 1990. Though Eastwood's award might have been some sort of belated recognition of his general contribution to the industry, it seems likely that the Academy would not have once again rewarded a film in such a low status genre unless there were a perception that *Unforgiven* was not 'just another Western', but a film which adopts some sort of thoughtful perspective on the genre.

Back in 1955, the eminent French critic André Bazin put forward the view that the classical Western had peaked around 1940, since when the genre had been burdened with something he called the 'sur-Western', defined as 'a Western that would be ashamed to be just itself, and looks for some additional interest to justify its existence – an aesthetic, sociological, moral, psychological, political, or erotic interest, in short some quality extrinsic to the genre and which is supposed to enrich it'.[37] Bazin's somewhat puritanical preference for the simplicities of the classical form, which also extends towards scepticism about whether CinemaScope could bring anything to the genre, is admirable in its way, but looks rather extreme now, and nearly fifty years on critical orthodoxy seems to place a special value on those films which can in some way add something to the genre, which are more than 'just' Westerns.

The term that is used over and over again in critical discussions of *Unforgiven* is 'revisionist'. In political discourse this tends to be a term of abuse, used of those who have deviated from the true path of revolutionary socialism. But in relation to *Unforgiven* it is used to describe with approval the film's apparent project of 'revising' the basic themes and conventions of the Western, which, it is assumed, have become both banal and backward-looking. The critical consensus is that *Unforgiven* runs counter to the traditional ideological drift of the genre, in particular with regard to its stance towards violence, which it strips of its glamour. Several commentators have remarked upon the deliberation with which the film intervenes in the history of the genre, taking on such topics as 'agrarian economy, capitalist enterprise and commodity ownership, law and law enforcement and their relation to moral order in the world, the place and value of women in a man's environment, and of course the nature and constitution of heroism on the frontier'.[38]

However, there's a certain amount of slippage in the use of 'revisionist', which sometimes is applied directly to *Unforgiven*, but other times to an earlier cycle of Westerns, originating in the 1960s and associated with Sam Peckinpah and Sergio Leone, which 'introduced a grungy realism of detail, embedded in cynical views of individual heroism and national ambition'[39] and of which *Unforgiven* is merely a late flowering example. Or perhaps *Unforgiven* represents a further modification of this trend, not as nihilist or cynical as the revisionist works, instead 'carefully supplying everyone with reasonable, carefully explicated motives for their behavior, but bringing them to bloody chaos anyway'; a kind of 're-revisionist' Western, in Richard Schickel's phrase.[40] But whether the film is

the last in a long line of such works, or represents something new (remember the script was originally written in the mid-1970s), there is near universal agreement that it aims to overturn the certainties of the classical form of the genre.

Opinions differ, however, on whether it succeeds. Does the last sequence of the film essentially recuperate whatever 'revisions' the film has made upon the conventions of the Western, when the 'reformed' William Munny transforms himself into a righteous avenger and a murderous killer? William Beard believes so, asserting that 'Even the most deconstructive Eastwood film (and *Unforgiven* probably is that) retains what is deconstructed: the transcendental-heroic Eastwood persona. The films do not supplant a heroic discourse with an anti-heroic one. Rather they present both, contradictory, discourses side by side.'[41] Paul Smith concurs: 'whatever kinds of revisionism are attempted (even if "truthful"), the mystified, mythological (and vicious) "spirit of the West" always returns. In other words, *Unforgiven* depicts the fiction returning in overpowering form to literally blow away the demythologizing truthfulness of the sheriff [as expressed in his testimony to W. W. Beauchamp].'[42]

Perhaps it would be asking a lot to expect a conclusion in which we witness William Munny facing up to the full implications of his volte-face, in which we are forced to share his despair at the betrayal of his wife in his drunken reversion to bloodshed. Hollywood does not often deal in such desolation. As it is, the ending in which Munny literally fades from the screen avoids the issue. The enigma with which Mrs Feathers is confronted is the audience's own. Munny's viciousness and his reformation cannot be reconciled.

Notes

1 Quoted in Christopher Frayling, *Spaghetti Westerns: Cowboys and Europeans from Karl May to Sergio Leone* (London: Routledge and Kegan Paul, 1981), p. 35.

2 In *All on Accounta Pullin' a Trigger*, a documentary issued with the Special Edition DVD of *Unforgiven*, its scriptwriter, David Webb Peoples, says that he had Glendon Swarthout's original novel, on which *The Shootist* was based, in mind when he wrote his own script.

3 In the 1990s, Kevin Costner has attempted to pick up the mantle, in *Dances With Wolves* (1990), *Wyatt Earp* (1994) and *Open Range* (2003), but the latter appears to confirm that only ironic or nostalgic Westerns are now possible.

4 That job has been adequately done elsewhere; see the Bibliography.

5 See Richard Slotkin, *Gunfighter Nation: The Myth of the Frontier in Twentieth-Century America* (New York: Atheneum, 1992).

6 See, for example, Sandra L. Myers, *Westering Women and the Frontier Experience 1800–1915* (Albuquerque: University of New Mexico Press, 1982) and Julie Roy Jeffrey, *Frontier Women: The Trans-Mississippi West* (New York: Hill and Wang, 1979).

7 In *The Searchers* Lars Jorgensen, having discovered the Indians have run off his cattle, exclaims: 'Next time I'll raise pigs, by golly!' But Lars is not the heroic type.

8 Will Wright, *Sixguns and Society: A Structural Study of the Western* (Berkeley: University of California Press, 1975).

9 See Richard Schickel, *Clint Eastwood* (London: Arrow Books, 1997), p. 461. Gene Hackman echoes this in the documentary, *All on Accounta Pullin' a Trigger*, claiming that Daggett is based on Darryl Gates, the LA police chief at the time of the Rodney King beating. This may be fanciful, but casting the black actor Morgan Freeman as Ned lends a certain plausibility to the contemporary reference.

10 Though not as insistently masochistic as Brando, Eastwood receives his fair share of beatings in his Westerns, including a fearsome whipping in *High Plains Drifter* (1972).

11 See Jim Pines's entry on 'Blacks' in Edward Buscombe (ed.), *The BFI Companion to the Western* (London: BFI/André Deutsch, 1988).

12 Michael Carlson, *Clint Eastwood* (Harpenden: Pocket Essentials, 2002), p. 72.

13 In a telephone conversation with the author, 8 January 2004.

14 Most of the exteriors of *Unforgiven* were shot on the E. P. Ranch in Alberta in Canada, sixty miles southwest of Calgary.

15 Walter Prescott Webb's book *The Great Plains* was first published in 1931.

16 Newspapermen, no less prone to mythologise than fiction writers, appear in John Ford's *Fort Apache* (1948) and *The Man Who Shot Liberty Valance* (1962). In an interview about *Unforgiven* Eastwood, in discussing the character of Beauchamp, quoted the celebrated if gnomic line from *Liberty Valance*: 'When the legend becomes fact, print the legend.' See Robert E. Kapsis and Kathie Coblentz, *Clint Eastwood: Interviews* (Jackson: University Press of Mississippi, 1999).

17 This change of accent is not signalled in the script.

18 When Alice asks Little Bill why he has beaten an innocent man, Little Bill replies, 'Innocent of what?' (a line included in the original script). Richard Schickel quotes George Steiner's remark that this is a perfect Kafkaesque moment. (Schickel, *Clint Eastwood*, pp. 459–60.)

19 See Schickel, *Clint Eastwood*, pp. 463–4.

20 A minor mystery is that when he practises shooting on his farm, Will fires right-handed, then later when he shoots at the cowboy he's left-handed.

21 Kapsis and Coblentz, *Interviews*, p. 189.

22 See the aforementioned documentary.

23 One of the things that distinguishes *Unforgiven* from most of Eastwood's other films is the strong casting. Before *Unforgiven* it was unusual for Eastwood to play against such dominating actors as Richard Harris, Morgan Freeman and Gene Hackman. Had Eastwood got to the point in his career where he felt confident enough for that? Several of his subsequent films have also featured major co-stars: John Malkovich (*In the Line of Fire*), Meryl Streep (*The Bridges of Madison County*), Kevin Costner (*A Perfect World*), Hackman again and Ed Harris (*Absolute Power*), James Garner, Tommy Lee Jones and Donald Sutherland (*Space Cowboys*).

24 Telephone conversation with the present author.

25 Even though in the event the film was rated R, meaning anyone under seventeen required an accompanying adult.

26 Christopher Frayling points out in his review of *Unforgiven* in *Sight and Sound* (October 1992) that Munny's children are called Will and Penny. *Will Penny* is the title of a revisionist Western from 1967 starring Charlton Heston as an impoverished and ageing cowboy. It's even been suggested that Penny Munny might have a reference to the hero's economic woes.

27 Patrick McGilligan, *Clint, The Life and Legend* (London: HarperCollins, 2000), p. 468. Peoples confirmed this in a telephone call to the present author.

28 In a telephone conversation Peoples said he thought Eastwood was actually playing the part as a forty-year-old, which rather undermines the theory that he deliberately held back till he was old enough.

29 McGilligan, *Clint*, p. 198.

30 David Thomson, *The New Biographical Dictionary of Film* (London: Little, Brown, 2002), p. 262.

31 Schickel, *Clint Eastwood*, p. 461.

32 Schickel writes: 'Henry Bumstead's set for Big Whiskey, the miserable little Wyoming county seat, circa 1880, where most of the action was staged, contained no false fronts. Its buildings were solidly, expensively rooted on this land; every structure was fully practical, and all of the film's interiors were made here, not on a sound stage.' Schickel, *Clint Eastwood*, p. 453.

33 This story is told in Christopher Frayling, *Sergio Leone: Something to Do with Death* (London: Faber and Faber, 2000), p. 137.

34 Eastwood was himself born in San Francisco, in 1930.

35 Kapsis and Coblentz, *Interviews*, p. 182.

36 *Hollywood Reporter*, 31 July 1992; *Variety*, 3 August 1992; *New York Times*, 7 August 1992.

37 See André Bazin, *What Is Cinema? Vol. II* (Berkeley: University of California Press, 1971), translated by Hugh Gray, pp. 150–1.

38 William Beard, '*Unforgiven* and the Uncertainties of the Heroic', *Canadian Journal of Film Studies,* vol. 3, no. 2, Autumn 1994, p. 51.

39 Pat Dowell, '*Unforgiven*', *Cineaste*, vol. 19, nos 2/3, December 1992, p. 72.

40 Schickel, *Clint Eastwood*, p. 455.
41 Beard, '*Unforgiven* and the Uncertainties of the Heroic', pp. 59–60.
42 Paul Smith, *Clint Eastwood: A Cultural Production* (Minneapolis: University of Minnesota Press, 1993), p. 268.

Credits

Unforgiven

USA
1992

Directed by
Clint Eastwood
Produced by
Clint Eastwood
Written by
David Webb Peoples
Director of Photography
Jack N. Green
Edited by
Joel Cox
Production Designed by
Henry Bumstead
Music Score by
Lennie Niehaus

© Warner Bros., Inc
Production Companies
Warner Bros. presents
a Malpaso production

Executive Producer
David Valdes
Associate Producer
Julian Ludwig
Production Associates
Matt Palmer
John Lind
Production Auditor
Michael Maurer
Production Accountants
Lynn Elston
Jeffrey Kloss
**Assistant Production
Accountant**
Sheila Aquiline
Production Co-ordinator
Penny Gibbs
**Sonora Unit Production
Co-ordinator**
Carol Trost
**Assistant Production
Co-ordinators**
Anisa Lalani
Cathy Yost
Production Manager
Bob Gray
**Sonora Unit Production
Manager**
David Valdes
Unit Manager
Lynne Bespflug
Location Manager
Rino Pace
Production Secretary
Loranne Turgeon
**Assistant to Clint
Eastwood**
Melissa Rooker
First Assistant Director
Scott Maitland

**Second Assistant
Director**
Bill Bannerman
Third Assistant Directors
Grant Lucibello
Tom Rooker
**Sonora Unit Second
Assistant Director**
Jeffrey Wetzel
Script Supervisor
Lloyd Nelson
Casting by
Phyllis Huffman
Canadian Casting
Stuart Aikins
Casting Assistants
Nadene Katz
Bill Haines
'A' Camera Operator
Stephen St. John
'B' Camera Operator
Roger Vernon
**First Assistant
'A' Camera**
Anthony J. Rivetti
**First Assistant
'B' Camera**
Doug Craik
**Second Assistant
'A' Camera**
Marco Ciccone
**Second Assistant
'B' Camera**
Dan Heather
**Sonora Unit
2nd Assistant Camera**
Mark Anderson
Sonora Unit Loader
Peter Green

Key Grip
Charles Saldana
Best Boy Grip
Randy Swanson
Sonora Unit
Best Boy Grip
Hal Nelson
Dolly Grip
Carey Toner
Sonora Unit Dolly Grip
T. D. Scaringi
Chief Lighting Technician
Tom Stern
Assistant
Chief Lighting Technician
Jim Gregor
Sonora Unit Assistant
Chief Lighting Technician
Victor Perez
Still Photographer
Bob Akester
Special Effects
Co-ordinator
John Frazier
Special Effects Foreman
Maurice Routely
Sonora Unit Special
Effects Best Boy
Hal Selig
Assistant Film Editor
Michael Cipriano
Art Directors
Rick Roberts
Adrian Gorton
Set Designer
James J. Murakami
Set Decorator
Janice Blackie-Goodine
Property Master
Edward Aiona

Assistant Property
Masters
Michael Sexton
Dean Goodine
Sonora Unit Assistant
Property Master
Chuck McSorley
Construction
Co-ordinator
Jan Kobylka
Sonora Unit Construction
Co-ordinator
Ron Trost
Construction Foreman
Bruce Robinson
Standby Painter
George Griffiths
Head Painters
Doug Wilson
Gary Ripley
Wardrobe Department
Head
Glenn Wright
Men's Wardrobe
Supervisor
Carla Hetland
Women's Wardrobe
Supervisor
Joanne Hansen
Sonora Unit Set
Costumer
Valerie O'Brien
Head Make-up Artist
Mike Hancock
Assistant Make-up Artist
Stan Edmonds
Head Hair Stylist
Iloe Flewelling
Sonora Unit Hair Stylist
Carol Pershing

Titles and Opticals by
Pacific Title
Colour Timer
Phil Downey
Music Editor
Donald Harris
Scoring Mixer
Bobby Fernandez
Soundtrack
'Claudia's Theme' by
Clint Eastwood
Sound Mixer
Rob Young
Sonora Unit Sound Mixer
Michael Evje
Boom Operator
Kelly Zombor
Re-recording Mixers
Les Fresholtz
Vern Poore
Dick Alexander
Supervising Sound
Editors
Alan Robert Murray
Walter Newman
Sound Editors
Neil Burrow
Gordon Davidson
Marshall Winn
Butch Wolf
Cindy Marty
Assistant Sound Editors
Michael Mirkovich
Kimberly Nolan
Michael Ruiz
Negative Cutter
Donah Bassett
Supervising Dialogue
Editor
Karen Spangenberg

Dialogue Editors
James Issacs
Karen G. Wilson
ADR Supervisor
Devon Curry
Foley
Taj Soundworks
Technical Consultant
Buddy Van Horn
Transportation Co-ordinator
Keith Dillin
Transportation Captain
Ray Breckenridge
Transportation Co-captain
Randy Luna
Craft Service/First Aid
Rose Johnson
Sonora Unit First Aid
Diane Anderson
Sonora Unit Craft Service
Robert J. Groff
Caterer
Filmworks Catering
Sonora Unit Caterer
Tony's Food Service
Knives Designed by
J. P. Moss
Head Wrangler
John Scott
Wrangler Bosses
Tom Bews
Tom Glass
Tom Eirikson
Unit Publicist
Marco Barla

The Producers Gratefully Acknowledge the Invaluable Help and Co-operation of
Bill Marsden, Film Commissioner of Alberta; Murray Ord, IATSE 312 and the citizens of Brooks, Drumheller, High River and Longview, Alberta for their support and friendship during the production of this film
Dedicated to
Sergio [Leone] and Don [Siegel]

Cast
Clint Eastwood
William 'Bill' Munny
Gene Hackman
Little Bill Daggett
Morgan Freeman
Ned Logan
Richard Harris
English Bob
Jaimz Woolvett
The 'Schofield Kid'
Saul Rubinek
W. W. Beauchamp
Frances Fisher
Strawberry Alice
Anna Thomson
Delilah Fitzgerald
David Mucci
Quick Mike
Rob Campbell
Davey Bunting
Anthony James
Skinny Dubois

Tara Dawn Frederick
Little Sue
Beverley Elliott
Silky
Liisa Repo-Martell
Faith
Josie Smith
Crow Creek Kate
Shane Meier
Will Munny
Aline Levasseur
Penny Munny
Cherrilene Cardinal
Sally Two Trees
Robert Koons
Crocker
Ron White
Clyde Ledbetter
Mina E. Mina
Muddy Chandler
Henry Kope
German Joe Schultz
Jeremy Ratchford
Deputy Andy Russell
John Pyper-Ferguson
Charley Hecker
Jefferson Mappin
Fatty Rossiter
Walter Marsh
barber
Garner Butler
Eggs Anderson
Larry Reese
Tom Luckinbill
Blair Haynes
Paddy McGee
Frank C. Turner
Fuzzy
Sam Karas
Thirsty Thurston

Lochlyn Munro
Texas Slim
Ben Cardinal
Johnny Foley
Philip Hayes
Lippy MacGregor
Michael Charrois
Wiggens
Bill Davidson
Buck Barthol
Paul McLean
train person 1
James Herman
train person 2
Michael Maurer
train person 3
Larry Joshua
Bucky
George Orrison
'The Shadow'
Gregory Goossen
fighter

11,746 feet
130 minutes 31 seconds

Dolby
Colour by
Technicolor
2.35:1 [Panavision]
MPAA: 31757

DVD available from Warner
Home Video (2002)

Credits compiled by
Markku Salmi

Bibliography

This is not a complete listing but simply works that I found useful.

Books

Carlson, Michael, *Clint Eastwood* (Harpenden: Pocket Essentials, 2002)

Frayling, Christopher, *Sergio Leone: Something To Do with Death* (London: Faber and Faber, 2000).

————, *Spaghetti Westerns: Cowboys and Europeans from Karl May to Sergio Leone* (London: Routledge & Kegan Paul, 1981; 2nd edn, London: I. B. Tauris, 1998).

————, *Clint Eastwood* (London: Virgin Publishing, 1992).

Gallafent, Edward, *Clint Eastwood Actor and Director* (London: Studio Vista, 1994).

Kapsis, Robert E. and Kathie Coblentz, *Clint Eastwood: Interviews* (Jackson MS: University Press of Mississippi, 1999).

Kitses, Jim, *Horizons West: Directing the Western from John Ford to Clint Eastwood* (London: BFI Publishing, 2004).

Knapp, Lawrence F., *Directed by Clint Eastwood* (Jefferson NC: McFarland, 1996).

McGilligan, Patrick, *Clint: The Life and Legend* (London: HarperCollins, 2000).

Schickel, Richard, *Clint Eastwood* (London: Arrow, 1997).

Smith, Paul, *Clint Eastwood: A Cultural Production* (Minneapolis: University of Minnesota Press, 1993)

Articles

Babiak, Peter E. S., 'Rewriting Revisionism: Clint Eastwood's *Unforgiven*', *CineAction!* no. 46, June 1998.

Beard, William, '*Unforgiven* and the Uncertainties of the Heroic', *Canadian Journal of Film Studies* vol. 3 no. 2, Autumn 1994.

Combs, Richard, 'Shadowing the Hero', *Sight and Sound* vol. 2 no. 6, October 1992.

Dowell, Pat, '*Unforgiven*', *Cineaste* vol 19 nos. 2–3, December 1992.

Frayling, Christopher, '*Unforgiven*', *Sight and Sound* vol. 2 no. 6, October 1992.

Greenberg, Harvey R., '*Unforgiven*', *Film Quarterly* vol. 46 no. 3, Spring 1993.

Grist, Leighton, '*Unforgiven*', in Ian Cameron and Douglas Pye (eds), *The Movie Book of the Western* (London: Studio Vista, 1996).

Ingrassia, Catherine, 'Writing the West: Iconic and Literal Truth in *Unforgiven*', *Literature/Film Quarterly* vol. 26 no. 1, 1998.

Jameson, Richard T., 'Deserve's got nothing to do with it', *Film Comment*, Sept–Oct 1992.

Kelley, Susan M., 'Giggles and Guns: The Phallic Myth in *Unforgiven*', *Journal of Film and Video* vol. 47 nos. 1–3, Spring–Fall 1995.

Carl Plantinga, 'Spectacles of Death: Clint Eastwood and Violence in *Unforgiven*', *Cinema Journal* vol. 37 no. 2, Winter 1998.

Prats, Armando J., 'Back from the Sunset: The Western, the Eastwood Hero, and *Unforgiven*', *Journal of Film and Video* vol. 47 nos. 1–3, Spring–Fall 1995.

Sandow, John, 'Forgiving (Violence) and Forgetting (Women): Failed Revision in *Unforgiven*', *Focus* no. 17, 1997.

Sheehan, Henry, 'Scraps of Hope: Clint Eastwood and the Western', *Film Comment*, Sept–Oct 1992.

Thumim, Janet, '"Maybe He's Tough But He Sure Ain't No Carpenter": Masculinity and In/Competence in *Unforgiven*', in Pat Kirkham and Janet Thumim (eds), *Me Jane* (London: Lawrence & Wishart, 1995), reprinted in Jim Kitses and Gregg Rickman (eds), *The Western Reader* (New York: Limelight Editions, 1998).

Tibbetts, John C., 'Clint Eastwood and the Machinery of Violence', *Literature/Film Quarterly* vol. 21 no. 1, 1993.

Also Published

Amores Perros
Paul Julian Smith (2003)

L'Argent
Kent Jones (1999)

Blade Runner
Scott Bukatman (1997)

Blue Velvet
Michael Atkinson (1997)

Caravaggio
Leo Bersani & Ulysse Dutoit
(1999)

A City of Sadness
Bérénice Reynaud (2002)

Crash
Iain Sinclair (1999)

The Crying Game
Jane Giles (1997)

Dead Man
Jonathan Rosenbaum
(2000)

**Dilwale Dulhaniya Le
Jayenge**
Anupama Chopra (2002)

Don't Look Now
Mark Sanderson (1996)

Do the Right Thing
Ed Guerrero (2001)

Easy Rider
Lee Hill (1996)

The Exorcist
Mark Kermode (1997,
2nd edn 1998,
rev. 2nd edn 2003)

Eyes Wide Shut
Michel Chion (2002)

Heat
Nick James (2002)

The Idiots
John Rockwell (2003)

Independence Day
Michael Rogin (1998)

Jaws
Antonia Quirke (2002)

L.A. Confidential
Manohla Dargis (2003)

Last Tango in Paris
David Thompson (1998)

**Once Upon a Time in
America**
Adrian Martin (1998)

Pulp Fiction
Dana Polan (2000)

The Right Stuff
Tom Charity (1997)

**Saló or The 120 Days of
Sodom**
Gary Indiana (2000)

Seven
Richard Dyer (1999)

**The Shawshank
Redemption**
Mark Kermode (2003)

The Silence of the Lambs
Yvonne Tasker (2002)

The Terminator
Sean French (1996)

Thelma & Louise
Marita Sturken (2000)

The Thing
Anne Billson (1997)

**The 'Three Colours'
Trilogy**
Geoff Andrew (1998)

Titanic
David M. Lubin (1999)

Trainspotting
Murray Smith (2002)

The Usual Suspects
Ernest Larsen (2002)

The Wings of the Dove
Robin Wood (1999)

**Women on the Verge of a
Nervous Breakdown**
Peter William Evans (1996)

**WR – Mysteries of the
Organism**
Raymond Durgnat (1999)